The Student's Guide to Entrepreneurship

Marc Steren

Published by Millington House Publishing,
a division of Cosmic Stuff Media, LLC.
Bel Air, Maryland

ISBN-13: 978-1941616260
ISBN-10: 1941616267

Millington House Publishing

http://millingtonhousepublishing.com

TESTIMONIALS

An entrepreneurial mindset is a quality that leads to success in virtually any career. Marc has managed to translate his own entrepreneurial experience into a series of lessons that really help students understand the process and what it takes to be successful. He gives them both the inspiration and the tools needed to create a new venture - now or in the future.

> Alyssa Lovegrove
> Associate Director and Adjunct Professor
> Georgetown Entrepreneurship Initiative
> McDonough School of Business
> Georgetown University

After taking Mr. Steren's entrepreneurship capstone course I was admitted into the University of Maryland. During my first semester I was first runner up at a school wide pitch competition, I was accepted into the competitive student run incubator, and I was given permission to join the junior and senior level entrepreneurship development class due to my prior knowledge of entrepreneurship and the business model canvas. All of this I learned directly from Mr. Steren.

> Cody Branchaw
> University of Maryland student
> Co-Founder kanga Trash and Energy Systems

Your course helped me find the entrepreneurial spirit inside of me that I knew existed, but would not have found without taking the class.

Brian Kelley
Babson University student

I had the privilege of being a mentor in the program. I had the opportunity to observe Marc's incredible gifts as an educator. He seamlessly taught high school students graduate level material in a way that was cogent and easy to digest. His methods are unparalleled in setting a paradigm to achieve maximum results in a unique manner. Mr. Steren inspires, sets lofty goals in a manner that sets the student on a journey to achieve their dreams.

Jon D. Isaacson
Managing Director
American Capital Venture Capital

Marc has converted business concepts into a strong academic curriculum that engages students in every grade in the potential and excitement of entrepreneurship. Thanks to him, our students have learned that every idea has value, every plan benefits from feedback and that teamwork and collaboration are key to long-term success in today's global environment. Marc is a superstar amongst educators who wrote the guide on how to implement an exciting hands-on entrepreneurship program.

Dr. Jerry Boarman
Bullis Head of School

ABOUT THE AUTHOR

Marc Steren is the Director of Entrepreneurship at the Bullis School and the Co-Director of Georgetown University's Summer Launch Program, where he is an Entrepreneur-In-Residence. Marc is the winner of the National Federation of Independent Business Entrepreneur Educator of the Year 2015, and the David S. Stone Teaching Excellence Award, 2015. He has mentored and advised over 35 student entrepreneurship teams and is currently on the board of directors of MARK Spirit, a mobile application connecting millennial alumni and their high schools through social giving and donations.

SPECIAL THANKS:

To, Tami Levey, my editor, for dedicating her month of August to editing the book. You made some amazing changes and the book is better off for it.

To Jack Copeland, my research editor, for acting as a fantastic sounding board and providing wonderful insight from a student's perspective.

To my wonderful wife Stephanie, and kids, Ian, Jack and Logan. May all of your dreams come true since you have made all of my dreams come true.

And finally, to my wonderful parents. You taught me to live life with laughter and to not be afraid to take risks.

CONTENTS

THE STUDENT'S GUIDE TO ENTREPRENEURSHIP

Jordan and I "started" ZebraPass in my apartment in the late 1990's. By started, I mean to say we thought of a great business idea and had hoped to see it through to its fullest potential. We had been pitching our idea to promising investors for 6 months, to no avail. We were getting discouraged and were concerned that our idea would never take off.

We walked into the office of a well known angel investor with sweaty palms and our handy powerpoint presentation. Looking back, our concept now seems pretty commonplace: a person's cell phone would be embedded with an RFID chip (similar to a gym FOB), and when you attended any sports team event, you would merely wave your phone over the turnstile and out would dispense your ticket.

A major concern was for the stadium advertisers; where was their return on investment? If you merely placed a sign in the stadium, the actual returns were too fleeting to determine if the advertisement was worth it. Our software, however, solved that problem. After the game, the ticket holder would go to the sponsor, let's say Burger King, for example, swipe his phone on one of our "zpads" located in that particular retail location, and out would dispense a coupon, "Hey Marc, thanks for coming to the game, here is 10% off your whopper." The concept was designed for any ticketing event, so we thought the concept would work for movie theaters as well.

Which brings us back to our investor friend. He was offering me and Jordan $1 million for 50% of the company. Here was the catch: if we couldn't sign up half of the movie theater chains in the course of one year, David would control 55% of the company. We had one week to make up our minds. Jordan and I argued, and argued some more, on the way home from that meeting. The argument continued over the next few days. I wanted to take the deal, Jordan didn't. Finally, I relented and we decided to forgo the $1 million despite the fact we had nothing; no customers, no software, no nothing. We had a plan, we were two young entrepreneurs with a lot of chutzpah.

We decided to raise the $1 million as our seed money primarily from family and friends and a few targeted celebrities we thought could help us strategically down the road. We were raising the money to build the software and to get customers.

Our investors for the seed round included some neat investors: Steven Spielberg, Michael Jordan, Wayne Gretzky and Harris Barton from the 49ers.

And what did we do with the $1 million? We spent every last penny to build the most amazing software, with open APIs that could plug into any ticketing system. We had the NY Giants, Jacksonville Jaguars, and the Richmond Braves all signed up. We even had the movie chain Wallace Theaters signed up as well. The chain would eventually pilot our program to test movies.

We were also set to pilot the program with the Richmond Braves and that is when we struck what we thought was gold. We received a $4 million investment from Nokia Ventures Series A round. They brought in this amazing CTO and that was when we were finally able to spend. In fact, Nokia Ventures *told* us to spend. So instead of using our software platform that we had already built, we took everything in house and rebuilt it from scratch. Why test when you can spend? Over the next 18 months we spent, and spent, and how many pilot programs did we run since the Nokia Ventures investment? Zero. Before we knew it, we were out of money and being bought by another Nokia Venture company for pennies on the dollar.

I know now there was a better way than to just spend money. I came across Steve Blank's *The Start Up Manual*, Alexander Osterwalder's *Business Model Generation*, Ash Maurya's *Running Lean* and Eric Reiss' *The Lean Startup*, and it all clicked. What if we had piloted our ticketing system with the Braves, bugs and all, received feedback and iterated from there? What if, though sports tickets were an existing market, we had preserved cash as we entered the new market of mobile ticketing and loyalty systems? And of course, though we spoke to numerous sports teams, the so called "economic buyer," what if we spoke to more fans, the actual end users? What if we actually went out and followed Steve Blank's **customer development** and "identified the problem, tested the problem, tested the solution and then pivoted from there?"

I now teach entrepreneurship at Bullis High School and utilize a specific method of teaching entrepreneurship. I incorporate the valuable lessons of lean methodology and customer development and combine those lessons with the fundamental skill that is needed for all student entrepreneurs; a strong belief in themselves and their team. This book outlines this methodology, the "BACCA™" methodology, that I use to teach students. I am hopeful that students can pick up this book, be inspired, and become student entrepreneurs.

The challenge for high school and college teachers is to implement a systematic approach to entrepreneurship. At Bullis, we have developed the BACCA™ methodology to teach the fundamental tenements of entrepreneurship.

Belief
Association of Teams and Design Thinking
Canvas
Customer Development
Analytics

How to use this Book

Each chapter commences with a quick overview and goals. Though we articulated a formulaic methodology, please feel free to to use different portions of the program as needed.

Chapter 1

Belief: Improving the Psychology of the Student

Goal:
    Inspire students to believe in themselves.

Resources:
    Hill, N. (1987). Think and Grow Rich. New York: Fawcett Books.,
    Byrne, R. (2006). The Secret. New York: Simon and Schuster.
    Anthony Robbins. Retrieved July 17, 2015, from Tony Robbins website: https://www.tonyrobbins.com

Belief

Jordan, my co-founder and business partner, was traveling in Los Angeles with our technology officer in charge of hardware. They stopped by Nobu to grab some sushi when they noticed Wayne Gretzky having dinner with his lovely wife, Janet Jones. Jordan immediately swung into action, stood up and introduced himself to Wayne Gretzky. Jordan had so mastered his pitch and was so confident in himself and our idea that after a few minutes, Wayne handed him the card of his business agent, Lori Hunter, and said "call her."

So he did. It was Jordan's overwhelming belief in himself that gave him the confidence to give a pitch to one of the most famous athletes on the planet. It brings us to the question, how do we get that same belief that Jordan had?

In this chapter, we will explore threads of commonality between modern day motivational thought with historical methods and concepts. We will make evident the underlying truth that techniques of belief have existed for centuries and if followed, can provide a proven roadmap for success. It gives us the self confidence to believe in ourselves and our ideas.

Tony Robbins is one of the greatest motivational speakers today. Motivation, however, is fleeting. What makes Tony special is the strategies and techniques that he outlines in his program. All good sources of motivation come from two basic human emotions: pain and pleasure. It is the ability to utilize both the pain and pleasure, and knowing when to employ each emotion, that will help us develop a strategy.

I graduated from law school and had the good fortune of clerking for a wonderful judge and man, Paul H. Weinstein. I joined a law firm right after my clerkship ended and hated it. It wasn't so much that I hated the law, just the other attorneys. I learned that it was not for me, but I had to get to the pain point to know that I needed change. I became fully aware that I had hit this "pain" point when I was working on a pro bono case. I was headed out of town for vacation and I asked the opposing counsel if I could respond to her motion when I returned. She said "sure" so I went on vacation with a clear head knowing that I could address the motion upon my return. When I came back, there was a motion from the opposing counsel stating that I had failed to answer her previous motion so my defense should be dismissed.

I was in shock. I learned two important lessons. First, get things in writing. The second, and more important lesson for me, was that I needed to make a change in my life. This experience with opposing counsel was so painful that I decided it just wasn't worth it. I asked myself how to make a change in order to avoid the "pain." Change does not occur naturally, there needs to be intention for change to occur. How then, do we effectuate not just change, but real, positive change? There are the 4 P's to make this happen- pain, pleasure, passion and then, plan.

Pain

All change occurs in two phases, *initial change* and *everlasting change*.

Initial change occurs when you have hit rock bottom, when there is such massive pain you need to bring about the change. In other words, things have gotten so bad that we must seek alternatives.

Everlasting change is the change that occurs when that initial change becomes habitual.

Which is a more powerful emotion, pain or pleasure, and how shall we use each? The question ought not ask which is more powerful, but which is the starter and which is everlasting. Pain is the initiator - the causation that change must occur. The reward/pleasure helps maintain the desired change and makes it part of your daily life.

Pleasure

As indicated, pain is clearly just the strong starting point. But pain is only that, a starting point. How do you maintain longevity of change? You add the pleasure. There must be a reward for a job well done that will continue inspiring us to stick with the change. By making it pleasurable, you now make a one time change into a daily change. You will want to reward yourself because you want to maintain the habit that now creates pleasure.

Passion

How then do we convert a pain into a pleasurable experience with rewards? We can only make this conversion by understanding "why" we want to change. What is motivating me to make a lasting change? Money can be a driving force but it is usually not the main driver. For example, I promised the students in my class that I would lose 15 pounds in 3 months; I posed a challenge to myself. The "why" I intended to lose so much weight was to make sure that I am around to see all of the amazing things that my own children will accomplish as they continue to grow: college, their choice of careers, marriage, grandkids. I want to be around and be a part of their lives for as long as I can. It motivates me to get up every morning at 5:15 and exercise. The occasional twinkee is no longer for me, at least not anymore. I have found my "why" for change and because the why is a strong one, I am passionate about it. I have had the pain of being overweight, the "rock bottom" so to speak, and am starting to enjoy the pleasure of looking slim in my new me. It is pleasurable to see a skinny me, the compliments from friends allow me to feel rewarded for my efforts. And of course, I have the "why," the real passion of seeing my children grow older, that has inspired me to maintain this change.

Plan

Now that you have determined the pain to make a change, the pleasurable rewards, the passion or the "why" to make this change, you need a plan to implement the change. Without a real plan for success, you are lost. In future chapters, we introduce the **business model** canvas that acts as your plan for your business. For developing belief in yourself, we have created the "Hill Canvas" named after the famous author Napoleon Hill.

The Hill Canvas helps the student entrepreneur hold themselves accountable by putting your beliefs down in writing.

First, a little background on Napoleon Hill. He wrote the classic "Think and Grow Rich" and set forth an everlasting principle of how to be successful. Hill introduced the concept that "Thoughts become Things" and that the mind, just like any other muscle, could be strengthened through continual repetition of affirmations. Our Hill Canvas can be found at the end of the chapter. Here are the directions on how to use it.

In a clear and concise statement write down the following:

The *definite expected outcome* that you want to achieve. It must be specific!

The next sentence should be what you are *willing to give* in return for the outcome. In terms of a business model seeking profits, what work are you willing to commit yourself to in order to achieve this monetary amount.

The outcome, and the work needed to accomplish that amount, are both tied to a *definite date* for receiving that amount. It has to be a concrete date.

Once your Hill Canvas is filled out, student entrepreneurs should read it out loud twice a day, once in the morning and again just before you go to bed. When reading out loud the Hill Canvas, envision that you have already accomplished everything on it, really feel what it is like to have achieved it. In other words, don't think of the Hill Canvas as something that will occur tomorrow, but act as if it has already occurred. As Tony Robbins recommends, "Begin to live as though your prayers are already answered."

As stated above, the Hill Canvas represents your desired outcome. At first glance, there are many student entrepreneurs who may feel as if there is no way to achieve their goal. Let's use a simple example of a desired outcome as a long, 3 mile walk home from school. This expected outcome, the long walk home, can seem daunting and intimidating when looking at it from the beginning. By themselves, daunting tasks of achievements, such as a long walk home, can seem impossible. To avoid this "long walk" syndrome, i.e., fearing your own "big goal" that you have written down on the Hill Canvas, we must add smaller, intermittent goals or "baby steps" of achievement to get to that big goal. Along the way, with each achieved goal, the desired outcome becomes closer and closer. The attached **Copeland Goal Chart** sets forth a simple chart to measure both your big goal and the baby steps you need to achieve your desired goal. A simple chart that illustrates the long walk home with smaller, incremental goals. In addition, the baby step process instills positive habits to work towards every single day in order to achieve the ultimate, big goal.

So, how did Jordan's meeting go with Lori Hunter, Wayne Gretzky's business manager? As it turned out, Jordan was unable to attend it! Due to a death in his family, I filled in. I sat down with Lori Hunter and she told me I had 5 minutes to make the pitch. Despite her limited time, I ended up staying for a full hour, after which, she looked at me over the table and said,

"Wayne is in."

I had the confidence and self belief that we were on to something great. My confidence enabled me to convince others of the same. And how great was Wayne Gretzky? He took Jordan and me to a hockey game, mingled with professional athletes, and when he saw us he immediately called out our names and told us to join the rest of the gang. To this day, I can look back at that evening with real fondness.

The Hill Belief Canvas

Vision Photo	What You Are Willing To Give In Return For The Money	Clear and Concise Statement	Business Model Canvas
	Definite Date For Receiving The Money		Read Written Statement Twice Daily → See and Feel Already In Possession Of The Money Morning_____ Night_____
$ Definite Amount		Say Thank You	

Goal Chart:
Example:

Small Goals	Plan and map out with detail what the prototype will look like	Buy the supplies needed to make the prototype	Begin building the prototype	Make minor last minute adjustments and corrections to the prototype	Overall goal: Make a basic prototype of company's product.
Must be done by:	7/07/15	7/10/15	7/17/15	7/24/15	End date: 8/1/15
Actions needed to achieve goals	- Meet with team members to discuss the prototype - Draw a model of the prototype and revise throughout the week	- Use the diagram of the prototype from the last goal to make a supplies list and use that list and buy all necessary materials.	- Work with my team and use the materials to begin building the prototype	- Use the prototype to see where it needs work and where it is good. - Use that input to revise the prototype	
Finished	√	√	√		

Chapter 2

Association and Teams

Goals:

> Learn how to work within a team and to develop ideas, design thinking to spark the ideation process.

Resources:

> Maxwell, J. C. (2004). The 17 Indisputable Laws of Teamwork. Nashville: Thomas Nelson Publishers,
>
> Dyer, J., Gregersen, H., & Christensen, C. (2011). The Innovator's DNA: Mastering the Five Skills of Disruptive Innovators. Boston: Harvard Business Review Press

During ZebraPass, we had developed a real time mobile ticketing system that would tie directly into the back office of the sports team. We signed up the Richmond Braves and each ticket would be sold from the inventory, in real time, and as such, that particular ticket would no longer be available in inventory. Our newest CTO brought over by Nokia, started to bring in his team to implement the system. Before we knew it, the system that we had spent over a million dollars creating was being scrapped for a new system that would "block" off a certain section for our tickets.

Our new CTO also brought in a new project manager. This new project manager ran the IT team with a tyrannical hand. The IT staff was disheartened as they went on to build an inferior product.

The new CTO also brought in a new marketing director, despite the fact that we already had Sue Spielberg running marketing. Sue had opened doors to the biggest players in the world: Pepsi, Dreamworks, Universal Pictures. Pretty much any place we wanted to go, one phone call from Sue got us in. Sue was clean cut, charming, and just downright nice. The new marketing director was from Philip Morris and was basically a walking cigarette. Her clothes, hair, and most definitely her breath, all smelled like smoke. I remember a story she told us of her days at Philip Morris: instead of having bowls of candy in their offices and conference rooms, they just opened packs of cigarettes. We always thought she took that bowl of cigarettes and kept it in her office.

The new marketing director was disliked. She was mean, caustic, and I think the final straw was when she outsourced our logo production. We sat down at the unveiling of the new logo to see that our striped ZebraPass logo had been replaced by a coffee cup steam image. All for the not so cheap price of $25,000. It was frustrating to see our brand change, and in addition, we were spending money like it was going out of style. Jordan and I felt our company was starting to disintegrate because people in important positions were violating all of the rules of leadership. There was no buy in or feeling of significance from any new members but the select few in management. No one felt like they were contributing or that their ideas were being accepted by management. It was the beginning of the end for ZebraPass.

Based on this breakdown, I have learned that there are 4 laws of developing a good team and developing leadership. I call them the **4A's of Association**:

Aspire for something greater

Acquire great help

Assessments in place

Accountability

Association

Bullis runs a capstone initiative where we divide the class into small teams that are no greater than five people. In college, the university has the ability to pull members from different departments, with different skill sets. Ideally, this would ensure that team members bring diverse viewpoints. In the high school ecosystem, however, students generally are not as specialized so they will have many overlapping skills. For this chapter, when we refer to association, we are discussing team dynamics but we are also referring to "associating" (The Innovator's DNA), making sense of, and integrating novel inputs into a unique, innovative manner.

The ability to work within the team structures, setting expectations, and searching for that common goal is divided into the 4A's.

Aspire for something greater than you

If one individual team member succeeds, then only he wins, but there is no greater sense of accomplishment than accomplishments achieved within a team. It may sound trite, but the desire to be part of something greater than themselves will inspire individuals to do amazing things. Ensure that student entrepreneurs are aspiring for something greater than themselves by making sure that each individual is *significant* and is *contributing*. It sometimes becomes difficult to subordinate your goals and your needs to that of the team, but in order to have a successful team, this self sacrifice becomes a necessity. This is why a clear, definable greater goal must be set and be transparent to the entire team. Effective dashboards articulate obtainable goals that reward the entire team for milestones met. This notion of "big team goals" supplanting individual accomplishments will help the team remain focused and to work in a collaborative manner.

As discussed previously, students at Bullis are placed into teams. We attempt to place them in these teams based on their different skill sets. There are three main reasons to ensure that co-founders have different skill sets.

First, though all founders must be aware of all of the happenings within the start up, it is a lot easier to divide up labor if the students can contribute differently and according to their skill set and strengths. Secondly, diversity of perspective can improve the creativity and pivot process. And finally, a shared sense of accomplishment will continue to push the team beyond limited individual goals. It gives each team member a feeling of "significance" if they can contribute to the team in a meaningful and unique manner. By giving them a role that caters to their strength you will give them a bigger opportunity to make significant contributions. During our capstone program, one team, Pearl Toothpaste, incorporated all of the team members' varying inputs to develop a customizable toothpaste tablet. Each contribution was as significant as the next and contributed to them winning Bullis' first shark tank competition.

Acquire great people

As your enterprise continues to grow, the goal of hiring must be tied with the goal of hiring people who are better than you and who will work well in your team environment. Ask yourself, do they see the same desired outcome as you? Do they aspire to a goal greater than themselves? Adding superstars who don't work well with others will merely sink the morale of that particular division, or worse, the entire organization.

Assessments in place

In the school environment, this translates into actual due dates for particular benchmarks. For example, 15 interviews on problem/solution, or fit or a feedback sessions may be due on a specific date and graded. Even if there is no graded assessment, there still have to be specific goals and deadlines all laid out in a transparent dashboard so the entire team sees them and can accurately gauge the progress of the company.

Accountability

By giving out assignments for every team member and making those assignments visible for all to see, each team will ensure that every student entrepreneur is accountable to each other. At Bullis, we make the student entrepreneur team have an open dashboard which every team member can easily access.

One of last year's capstone teams, Kanga Trash Systems, gained some traction during the Bullis Entrepreneurship Capstone. It was a student led company that produced biodegradable trash bags placed under a sporting event seat so that fans could dispose of their trash during the ballgame in a mess free manner. The outside interest was so great in this idea that the team signed a lucrative agreement with a professional baseball team. One of the 4 members continued the venture at college where he won a grant during his school's pitch competition for operating expenses. Two members of the team, however, attended different colleges and stopped participating in the venture. They were no longer part of the team and, fortunately, the operating agreement explicitly stated what the consequences for lack of work were (loss of shares). This transparency ensured that only individuals who continued to contribute would be rewarded and those who did not contribute, were no longer part of the venture. A transparent dashboard kept them all aware of each other's contributions and kept everyone accountable.

Aspire for something greater	Acquiring Great people	Assessments in place	Accountability
The main goals you hope to achieve:	Who you have begun working with:	Upcoming assessments:	What you have done for your team in the last week:
How you will obtain these goals:	Their strengths and weaknesses:	How you will contribute to prepare for these assessments:	What more needs to be done:

Chapter 3

Design Thinking

Goals:

To learn to create and synthesize many ideas and concepts into one concept.

Resources:

[University of Maryland Page Promoting Innovation]. (n.d.). Retrieved July 14, 2015, from Academy for Innovation and Entrepreneurship website: http://innovation.umd.edu

[Stanford Design Program]. (n.d.). Retrieved July 14, 2015, from Stanford Design Program website: http://designprogram.stanford.edu http://www.smashingmagazine.com/2013/12/using-brainwriting-for-rapid-idea-generation/

In the beginning, Jordan and I would meet in Barnes and Noble and when that closed, we would head over to my apartment. Our brainstorming was free flowing and it was more by chance than by design. Our idea started with a simple problem: neither of us could stand waiting in line at the movies. We knew it was a problem that others shared because before long, there was a "solution" to deal with this problem. Specifically, Radiant Systems had set up kiosks in the theaters. You could call in your order and avoid the lines by going straight to the kiosks. But Jordan and I both found the kiosks inefficient, and we sometimes found ourselves waiting longer at these kiosks than the actual lines to purchase the tickets! There was no structure to our brainstorming, we just did it. Our ideas were not well refined and what we thought was a strength, I look back in hindsight and see as a clear weakness.

I have come to realize that design thinking is a technique, a skill that can be easily learned. There is a specific process that can enhance each design thinking session. As discussed in the previous chapter, association is the first step in making sure that you have a well rounded and diverse team to get as many ideas as you can. I am now going to discuss some key elements of design thinking; ideation, brainstorming, brainwriting, problem redefinition, and peer to peer ideations.

Ideation

Ideation is a creative process for generating as many ideas as possible and then filtering them down to the best ones.

In ideation, a useful tool for student entrepreneurs to help identify consumer problems is through **immersion** and empathy. In immersion, you place yourself in the very environment you are trying to find a solution for. In empathy, the focus is on observing the consumer and identifying their problems through behavioral observations. Some observations may be:

1. Seeing- what does the customer see through his eyes? What are his surroundings?
2. Hearing- what are the sounds, distractions of the city, the farm, the office, or whatever setting he may find himself in?
3. Saying- what is the person saying to his friends, to his parents, co-workers, or to you?
4. Doing- what are his actions? Do they contradict what he actually says?
5. Thinking- what is the potential customer thinking about? It is a lot easier to gauge one's thoughts as many will display them on their sleeves, so to speak, through social media. Look carefully at their facebook pages, instagram, blogs, and twitter accounts.

These observations will help develop a product that is tailored to the customer and that will best solve their problems.

Brainstorming

The immersion and observations will help with the brainstorming. In brainstorming, we set up two large boards. The first board is labeled "problems" and the second board is labeled "solutions." Student entrepreneurs place "problem" post-it notes on the problem board. Again, at this point we are trying to identify as many problems as possible. We then place the corresponding "solution" post-it notes on the solution board. In order to make sure that the problem post-its match with a corresponding solution post-it, place a small number in the upper left corner of the problem post-it and the corresponding solution post-it , so the problem and solution notes match. You can have more than one solution for a corresponding problem.

There are some basic rules for brainstorming:
1. Defer Judgment- there is no such thing as a bad idea.
2. Go for Quantity- we want to present as many possible problems and as many possible solutions as possible.
3. Encourage Wild ideas- this is the time to be creative and to enjoy the process.
4. Build on ideas- if you like an idea that a teammate puts on the board, feel free to add to that idea.
5. One conversation at a time- focus on problems first, and then go to the solutions to solve each problem presented.
6. Be visual- make sure to write all of the ideas on the post-its but feel free to make drawings or any other visuals you want to post on the board.
7. Headline- provide short, precise "headline" ideas so that everyone on the team can understand clearly and succinctly the idea presented.

Design thinking does not end after you have settled on a specific concept. Instead, the testing process and observation techniques are still necessary tools once the MVP testing, a concept we dive into in later chapters, has begun. ZebraPass launched a small pilot program with Wallace Theaters where consumers could order their movie ticket online and then use their RFID ZebraPass card at the theater to redeem their ticket. We should have been monitoring and observing the user experience from the time they ordered, to after redemption of the ticket-the whole experience. We should have gone to the problem and solution boards and, based on the observations of our consumers, refined the product contingent upon these observations.

Brainwriting

Brainwriting is a nice alternative to brainstorming as it alleviates some of the anxiety of coming up with ideas and then placing them on the board in front of your peers. The concept behind brainwriting is simple; present one problem and then have each team member write a possible solution on their own piece of paper. After a few minutes, everyone must pass their piece of paper to one of their teammates and they write on their teammates' solution paper. The new possible solution can be an add-on to their team's solution or an entirely new solution. This process is repeated 3 or 4 times.

Another advantage of brainwriting is that everyone is required to participate the same amount. In brainstorming, there may be one or two individuals dominating the process but in brainwriting there is equal participation. In addition, many ideas are generated because each time the paper is placed in front of you, you have to come up with an idea. The clear disadvantage is that the excitement of brainstorming and active participation is lost during brainwriting. You must decide which is best for your group.

Problem Re-definition

Sometimes it is important to redefine the problem. This process makes you search for alternatives. The process is fairly simple. First, identify a problem and replace 3 of the important words from the sentence with 8-10 alternatives.

example: We want to sell insurance to Bullis. replace 3 words

Alternatives

We

Sell

Bullis

We	Sell	Bullis
Sales force	give	students
students	license	teachers
friends of Bullis	test run	high school
administration	promote	private school
Board members	reward	all-girls schools
teachers	co-market	Bullis alumni
customer service	network	parents
policy holders	incentivize	coaches

Peer to Peer Ideation

With the advent of peer to peer software and the sharing economy, ideas that in the past merely solved a problem take on social components that enable the ideas to grow exponentially.

In peer to peer ideation, student entrepreneurs are challenged to convert their ideas to peer to peer, or as part of the shared economy. One approach is to show the Napster documentary, which tells the story of the rise and fall of the music sharing site Napster. After seeing the transition from merely solving the problem of having a better MP player, to socially connecting millions of people through music sharing, its the student entrepreneurs turn to attempt to make the transition.

For example, in the Bullis capstone, one team wanted to solve the problem of posting their videos and pictures online. After watching the videos, the company pivoted to a theme sharing collage where anyone can add their video or picture to a particular theme to share in producing a collaborative picture or video, thus leading this new company, PicShare, into a company that merely solved a problem to a more powerful, socially connecting, peer to peer picture or video sharing company.

Chapter 4

Teaching the Business Model Canvas and the Lean Stack

Goal:
> Understanding how to use the business model canvas.

Resources:
> Blank, S., & Dorf, B. (2012). The Startup Owner's Manual: The Step-By-Step Guide for Building a Great Company. K & S Ranch.,
> Osterwalder, A., & Pigneur, Y. (2010). Business Model Generation. John Wiley & Sons.

While large corporations are in the execution and operations stages, startups are still "discovering" a business model they can scale. Agility, speed, and decisiveness are just a few of the advantages that a start up has over a large corporation. Due to this constant fluidity, startups need a model that captures this "discovery" mode. There are two dynamic, one page models that work well with young startups. The first is Alexander Osterwalder's Business Model Canvas and the second is Ash Maurya's **Lean Canvas**. Though I use both in conjunction, the business model canvas acts as the foundation and the Lean Canvas is more of a complementary source to fill in the blanks.

The business model canvas is designed for the students to put "guesses" into every block of the canvas. Each guess or **"hypothesis"** needs to be phrased concisely and there should only be one or two guesses per block. From there, it is the entrepreneurs' job to go and validate or invalidate these guesses. The process of validating these guesses is called **customer development**, coined by Steve Blank. Customer development essentially calls for the students to get out of the building and interview potential customers and incorporate the feedback into their business model.

For my students, I refer to customer development as customer collaboration because the solutions are derived by consumer insights into their problems and possible design of the solutions. But instead of jumping into customer collaboration as suggested by Blank, I prefer to build a step by step process so the students understand every component of the canvas and simultaneously learn how to conduct interviews.

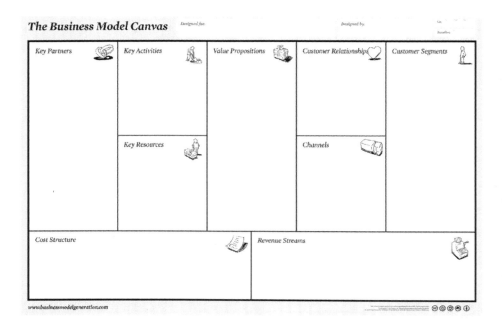

The business model canvas taken from
https://experiencinginformation.files.wordpress.com/2011/07/business_model_canvas.png

Chapter 5

Value Proposition in the Business Model Canvas

Goal:

> To understand that value propositions either solve a problem, socially connect people, or perform a job to be done.

Resources:

> Blank, S., & Dorf, B. (2012). The Startup Owner's Manual: The Step-By-Step Guide for Building a Great Company. K & S Ranch.
>
> Jobs to be Done. (n.d.). Retrieved July 8, 2015, from Clayton Christensen Institute for Disruptive Innovation website: http://www.christenseninstitute.org/key-concepts/jobs-to-be-done/

A value proposition is the service or benefit that you are providing to the customer.

Value propositions answer one of 3 basic questions:
1. Does your solution solve a problem? (Blank)
2. Does it fulfill a social need? (Blank)
3. What job does the consumer want done? (Christensen)

Problem/Solution determination- traditionally, young entrepreneurs would develop solutions and try to discover a market for those specific solutions. I prefer Ash Maurya's approach from Running Lean where we actually reverse the process: entrepreneurs identify consumer's problems and then find a solution to solve those specific problems. Maurya calls this the "problem/solution" fit stage. Though it seems fairly intuitive, by focusing in on the consumer's problems, the entrepreneur is forced to build products consumers actually want and is therefore more likely to develop a successful product.

In the end, the consumer only cares about their own problems; your solution is merely the resolution to their problems.

But not all problems rank equally to consumers. For example, a dull headache for a busy individual may not be important enough to seek out an immediate solution. A migraine, however, is a problem that needs to be solved right away. The person with a migraine is probably desperately seeking relief. They want a solution and they want it now. It is this "desperate" consumer that we are trying to identify. These **"early adopters"** who have identified a massive problem so prevalent that they will do anything to resolve it and are willing to take a chance on a start up.

How do we identify people that are "desperate" for your solution? During the customer discovery phase, look for individuals that are utilizing ad hoc solutions to their current problems. One of the startups in last year's Bullis program, CheckitOut, developed a mobile application that when you walked into a grocery store, a map would populate with step by step directions for each grocery item on the consumer's grocery list. How did the students know that Giant or any other grocery store might be interested in that solution? It was evident in the ad hoc solutions that Giant was already using to solve that specific problem. Customers that enter a grocery store can find large placards with many grocery items and their corresponding locations in the grocery store. A clear ad hoc solution to the distinct problem of finding grocery items. At this stage, the consumer, Giant grocery store, is desperate to find a solution to their problem. The magic happens when you convince the consumer to use your solution, and what better way to have them use your solution than to involve them in the process of determining exactly what that solution is. We will dive deeper into that during the customer collaboration section. Suffice it to say, discovering the specific problem is the first step in the process.

MVP

Many companies can provide products with numerous features and benefits to the consumers. Startups with limited resources, however, must stay focused on one feature that consumers are willing to pay for on day one.

We do want the students to list as many product features as possible, developing a product feature list. From there, however, we want them to hone in on the one feature that they can sell on day one. This feature is called the **minimum viable product**, or MVP. Focusing on the MVP enables us to test quickly and to not waste money on a lot of features that consumers may not want. Instead, validate or invalidate this main feature to determine whether or not a product or service can be built around it. This MVP should not be confused with being a cheaper version of your main product. Nathan Furr and Jeff Dyer state it best in "Innovator's Method" when they advise that the one feature be the "Minimum Awesome Product." It has to be good enough to win over those early adopters.

At ZebraPass, we were focused on providing mobile ticketing and loyalty systems. When Nokia Ventures brought in the new CTO, he wanted us to expand the concept to Starbucks and every retail location in the DC metropolitan region and beyond. We didn't stay focused on our MVP, and therefore drifted beyond our core business.

As you continue to test your MVP, you are trying to discover your true value proposition. There are many types of value propositions. In Business Model Generation: Strategyzer, Osterwalder lists nine basic value propositions. This is merely exemplary and not meant to be an exhaustive list of value propositions, but it is a wonderful place to see if your value proposition falls under one of those categories.

Many companies set out to find a solution for a specific problem. Your solution will serve as the value proposition. Good companies become great, however, when they can convert this solution into a social need that connects people. If I have a headache, I will seek out a treatment to relieve my headache, such as taking an aspirin. But once that headache is resolved, the treatment that I was so desperately seeking a little while ago, is no longer in my thoughts. Conversely, a company like Facebook that is socially connecting consumers will have consumers using that product multiple times a day, not just when they seek treatment. For these socially connected customers, using Facebook is an absolute social need.

Are socially connected companies limited to the Facebooks and the Twitters of the world? No, not necessarily. For example, Chipotle and Apple have connected with consumers so much so that their consumers have become raving fans and feel connected to their brands, respectively. Being connected to these brands becomes part of the consumers' social identity. There is a strong desire to eat at Chipotle. There is a need to buy only Apple products. Connecting with your customer is critical to growing a large business. Humans crave social interactions. So, it stands to reason that companies that can tap into this human need to connect will develop larger and more successful products than those that merely solve a problem.

If you ask people when was the last time they treated a headache, some may be hard pressed to answer. If you ask when was the last time they were on Facebook, almost every single person will admit they had been on multiple times during the day. The social component speaks volumes!

Fatcat, a start up in the Georgetown University Summer Launch Program, is a company that aggregates salaries for federal employees. It solves the problem for federal employees seeking raises and assists in the application process for another federal position at a different department. The software gives the user the resources and the power to negotiate a better wage. Fatcat, through numerous customer interviews with potential users of their website, discovered that after the employees had successfully negotiated a salary they would stop visiting their site; their problem had been solved. But the interviews also determined that federal employees felt disconnected from each other. What was occurring in the Department of Commerce was not being connected to the events that were transpiring at the Department of Agriculture. Due to the feedback and input from users, Fatcat discovered that by converting this problem/solution fit into a portal that could socially connected federal employees, they were on to a potentially significantly larger business.

Another approach to value proposition is stated by Chris Christensen. He asks the question, "what job or function did the consumer hire your product to do?" Christensen goes on to say, "With an understanding of the "job" for which customers find themselves "hiring" a product or service, companies can more accurately develop and market products well-tailored to what customers are already trying to do." - See more at: http://www.christenseninstitute.org/key-concepts/jobs-to-be-done/#sthash.7Qi067tb.dpuf

Christensen's approach understands that the same product may serve a different function for different customer segments. For example, an iPhone may serve as a certain status symbol for one segment while having more of a functional use for a different customer segment. The fundamental question to ask, "what job did that customer segment hire this product to do" will help young startups help iterate to a better solution.

Develop a product feature list below of at least seven features
1.
2.
3.
4.
5.
6.
7.

Now begin to eliminate one at a time and see what you remain with.

What is your MVP?

Chapter 6

Customer Segments

Goal:
> To identify and focus on a small segment of early adopters.

Resources:
> Blank, S., & Dorf, B. (2012). The Startup Owner's Manual: The Step-By-Step Guide for Building a Great Company. K & S Ranch.
>
> Maurya, A. (2012). Running Lean: Iterate from Plan A to a Plan That Works (Lean Series). Sebastopol: O'Reily Media.
>
> Osterwalder, A., & Pigneur, Y. (2010). Business Model Generation. John Wiley & Sons.

The **customer segment** block is a systematic step by step approach to identifying the early adopter of consumers who are going to buy your product. The first step is to write down the guess or "hypothesis" based on what you envision the the consumer gains from your product, or the pain being relieved by your product. The second step is to rank the importance of each of these to the consumer. The third step is to determine if there are any barriers to adopting your product. The fourth step is to identify the different types of consumers. The fifth step is to determine if there is product market fit, i.e., a match between the value proposition being offered and the customer segment, and finally, an analysis of what type of competitive market you just entered.

Let's examine each of these steps individually:

1. Hypothesis

At this stage, we are only guessing as to who the customer is. But that's ok. We are going to determine if we are correct or incorrect once we have completed the customer discovery process. It is important at this point to make guesses at to whom we think we are targeting and to write it down. Don't leave this blank.

2. Rank the problem/gain

As we have seen previously, though the consumer may perceive something as a problem, it may not be extreme enough for them to actually care about it, or care to seek out a solution. Part of the process is discerning which problems really concern the consumer. By resolving the extreme problems rather than the mild ones, you convert casual consumers into raving fans.

Societal gains

Societal gains can be categorized into either functional, social, or emotional gains for the consumer which enables them to connect with others. A wheelchair can be seen as a functional gain for the disabled. It may or may not increase a person's overall emotional well being, but it clearly enables the consumer to function, where as before his ability to get around had been diminished.

The interconnectivity of Facebook or Twitter is a social gain. The consumer does not need Facebook to function but may need to use Facebook to connect socially to other human beings. As stated previously, humans are social creatures by nature; therefore social media products tap into this powerful need for connection. Emotional connection companies that tug at our heart-strings, such as love (match.com), or sadness (a Nicholas Sparks book), are powerful emotions that can also present enormous opportunities. Emotional/ self-help books and increasing well being seminars are a thriving industry for an important reason; we want to tap into these powerful emotions to feel better. Many successful products and services tie into these consumer emotions.

Snapchat was developed by a few Stanford students. They initially called their company "picaboo" and today many people think Snapchat is used to send inappropriate, short, videos. The vast majority of snapchats, however, are of the goofy variety, created to provoke a chuckle, forging a real connection with other people. Not merely solving the problem of sending a short video, Snapchat connects two people with little effort.

In contrast, determining the consumer's pain allows us to construct solutions that act as "relievers." For example, the need to automate and make it easier to keep track of your accounting books led to Quickbooks and other accounting software programs. The pain of keeping your books was relieved with the advent of these programs.

3. Barriers to adopt your solution for the customer

In determining if consumers can adopt your product, ask if they are already committed to using your competitor's solution through either money, technology, or legislative lock in.

Let's take a more careful look at these lock ins. First, money. When you sign a contract with your wireless provider, there is usually a 2 year commitment. If you leave the contract prior to the two year period, there is an exorbitant exit fee that makes switching carriers quite costly. What looked like a great deal when you signed the initial contract with the carrier, now becomes a lock in due to the exit fee. In some instances, the amount is so draconian that the consumer ends up staying with that carrier.

The second major lock in is technology. Many consumers pair products from the same brand to have a seamless experience. Consumers of an Apple mac, for example, tend to buy the iPad mini and the Apple iPhone enabling the Apple iCloud to sync all of the consumer's books, music, and more, to each of those devices. This is an example of how technology can act as a lock in.

Another possible barrier is legislative. Congress, or a local municipality, may try to protect an incumbent's turf. This has played out in the "taxi wars" that Uber has had in almost every major city it has tried to enter. Taxi unions and their supportive legislative partners have tried to block or deter Uber from entering their area. This tactic has backfired as Uber tends to use this anti-competitive behavior to their advantage. Most Americans want to support free enterprise, and clearly Uber has been rewarded by facing down their legislative threats.

So, what did the ZebraPass consumer look like? I had no idea. I raised $5 million without knowing exactly who my customer was. I had no idea, nor had I even guessed, at what their pains and gains were. I certainly didn't go out and try to rank their problems. I merely built a solution and since I did not know who my consumer was, I squandered million of dollars in the process.

4. *Market Types*

Steve Blank in The Start Up Manual identified 4 markets that consumer segments reside in: new, clone, existing, and segmented. In a new market, you have a new product so customers and competitors are unknown. Since you are a first mover in this market, Blank provides some sage advice- hold on to your money until the market is ready to adopt your technology. In new markets, you are going to need that money to educate the market.

A clone market is merely bringing a successful product from one region to another region and trying it there. For example, bringing a successful KFC chain from the United States to China. There are a few challenges that you must be weary of in a clone market. First, customs may be different. So a KFC in China may have to adopt their product to the tastes of the Chinese consumer. Second, the laws in the new region may be different than the laws of the original market. Surely zoning laws in China are going to be different from those in downtown New York. In the clone market, customers are not as certain, but you would know who the competitors are.

In an existing market, you will know who the customers are since they have been using products similar to yours for a while. In addition, you will find well established competitors in this market. It is very difficult to compete in this market as the established players are entrenched and have brand following; unless of course, you can segment the market to find a particular niche. I find this to be the best way to attack an existing market, to segment it. Segmenting a market is a strategy whereby a broad target market is broken into subsets, allowing you to focus on a smaller and tighter niche.

5. *Product market fit*

The value proposition has to fit the correct customer segment. A wonderful example of a **product market fit** is the recent release of the iphone 5c and 5s models. Traditionally, iPhones would be released one model at a time, but with the iPhone 5c and 5s simultaneous release, Apple decided to bifurcate the market into two distinct customer segments. The iPhone 5c, plastic, colorful, and lower in price, has a product market fit for younger purchasers. The phone became an instant success with the high school market. The iPhone 5s, on the other hand, came in the more traditional colors, had a titanium back, and was listed at a higher price despite having many of the same features as the 5c. The customer segment for 5s matched the business consumer, making it a perfect product market fit as they could also afford to pay for it. On the contrary, an example of a poor product market fit would be a nursing home building a mobile application for their residents. This is a poor choice as often times senior citizens tend to be less tech savvy, and therefore would not use the mobile app.

6. Understanding the role of the customer in the purchase chain

It is important to know the roles that consumers have in the purchase chain. Many transactions will have 4 major players helping to determine whether there is going to be a purchase or not. Those players are the user, the influencer, the saboteur, and the economic buyer. Sometimes, one person can play multiple roles but it is important to understand their perspective and their motive for the transaction.

a. **The User**- the individual who actually uses the product. This may or may not also be the same individual who makes the purchase as well. His motive is simple, they must be satisfied with the product.

b. **The Influencer**- this individual helps influence the user in deciding to use the product.

c. **Saboteur**- this individual may feel threatened by the purchase, and therefore attempts to stop the purchase. This is different from a competitor, who is not part of the purchase chain, but instead is competing for the same sale.

d. **Economic Buyer**- the individual who pays for the purchase but may or may not be the actual user.

There are two main illustrative examples used to help explain the different players; business to consumer sale and the business to business sale.

Business to consumer: Little Joey (age 12) wants to buy the latest video game that his best friend Bob has. His mom has agreed to pay for it but his Dad is against little Joey playing video games, so is therefore against the purchase. He thinks it rots his brain, imagine that!

> Joey=user
> Bob=influencer
> Dad=saboteur
> Mom=economic buyer

Business to business example: Sara has a great software product that she wants to sell to Company Booyah. The software is designed to be used by the VP of Sales to automate his reporting capability. The CTO loves the product because it would make his job easier through streamlined reports. The software would eliminate ½ of the sales force. The CFO, in the end, would write the check and sign off on the purchase of the software.

> user= VP of Sales
> Influencer=CTO
> Saboteur=anyone on the salesforce, since they potentially could lose their job
> economic buyer=CFO

In the end, you must be cognizant of who you are trying to sell your product to. Are they the end user? Are they threatened by your product and therefore might try to sabotage the sale? By effectively understanding each player in the purchase chain, you are increasing your odds for a sale.

Fit Chart

Your customer Segment	
Your distribution channel	
Your customer's preferred distribution channel (i.e online store, retail store, etc.)	
Your customer's problem	
Your problem/solution fit	
Your product market fit	

Draw your customer below entering your market. Also draw the user, the influencer, the saboteur and the economic buyer below and show their interactions.

Chapter 7

Product Positioning

Goal:

Learn to position your product as a start up.

Resources:

Ries, A., & Trout, J. (2001). Positioning: The Battle for Your Mind. McGraw-Hill Education.

Consumers are inundated with choices. The numerous options available means that startups must be continually seeking ways to differentiate their offering from their competitors. This means that as you begin to target your customer segment you must also simultaneously consider how you are going to position your product within that customer segment.

In "Positioning," the authors contend that the best method of attack is to be the "first mover" in the space. This will help ensure that you are first in people's mind. There are many problems with this contention, from the point of view of a start up. There is a significant educational cost with being first. Consumers don't know your product, so therefore there are costs associated with educating the market on how to use your product. Generally, money is not a luxury that most startups have.

Moreover, the reality for most startups is that you are not the first to market. In these markets, they may not know your specific product or your brand, but there are similar products from your competitors. So how do we put your product "first" in the mind of consumers if you are not first to market? Here are the basic steps to help position your product.

1. Simplify your message- If the customer cannot understand what your product does in a few words, your messaging is too

complicated. Keep it simple and the message will be easier to remember.

2. Social connection- Companies are always looking to "connect" with their consumer. They are more than just selling the consumer a product, they are selling them a brand- something they can trust.

3. Position your product the way you see it- Chipotle is known as the healthier option for fast food. They have accomplished this with their promotion of organic products. If you look at the fat content of the Chik-fil-a grilled chicken and the Chipotle chicken, would you be surprised as to which has the higher fat content? It's all how you are positioning your product, don't let the competitor define who you are.

4. Reposition the competitor- This is a tactic used effectively by many consumer products. The focus will be on all of the negative qualities of your competitors. You are defining what your competitor is, and relative to this description of your competitor, you can place your product in a positive light.

5. Know your ranking- If you are number 2 or 3 in the market, the repositioning of your competition is the stronger strategy. If, however, you are the leader in the market, it is a better tactic to not refer to your competitor at all. There is always a constant battle for first place in the consumer's mind. There is no reason to give your competitor a place at the table if there is no need. Instead, focus on your product alone.

While we were making our rounds, trying to make our initial angel raise, Jordan and I were in deep conversation with the Merv Griffin group. They were all set to invest in our company when the person leading the Griffin Group told us they could no longer invest in ZebraPass. When asked why, the Merv Griffin Group told us that Ticketmaster saw us as a threat and as an inferior product. Ticketmaster had repositioned us even though we didn't see ourselves as a competitor. In the end, it didn't matter, the damage was done and they never made the investment in ZebraPass.

Positioning Chart

Other competitors in the market	
Your ranking amongst these competitors	
How your product is different from your competitors' product and how you will show that to your consumer	
How you are going to reposition your competitor	
How you will build a social connection with your customers (i.e Facebook, Twitter, deals)	
The simple message used to describe your product	

Chapter 8

Branding

Goals:
>   Learn to distinguish and brand one product and multiple brand companies.

Resources:
>   Ries, A., & Trout, J. (2001). Positioning: The Battle for Your Mind. McGraw-Hill Education.

What's in a brand? Branding and positioning work jointly in placing your product into the minds of the consumer. The question arises, should I brand my product with a generic name or one that indicates to the consumer what my product does? Here are the factors that help determine the naming of your brand.

First, does your company have multiple products? If so, than a generic brand makes the most sense. Kraft Foods has many food products, philadelphia cream cheese, A1 steak sauce, and so forth. Each particular product may have an indicator of what that product does but the overall brand name, "Kraft foods" doesn't give any indication to the specific type of foods Kraft makes. It is only generic enough to give the consumer a sense as to what the company does. This gives the company flexibility to produce multiple food products and to expand.

If however, you are a single product company, its imperative that the brand be an indication of the functionality of the product itself. Don't make the consumer guess as to the function of your product. For example, is there any doubt as to the function of "careerbuilder.com?" Easy to brand, easy to understand. Even if you have never heard of careerbuilder.com, at least you can venture a guess as to what they do.

Be aware that there are limitations to the expansion of the brand when you brand the company with the specific name. All companies must make this choice when choosing their company name.

Noti, one of the teams from last year's Bullis entrepreneurship capstone, was a "friends locator and chat" service. The name gave no indication as to its function so the founders were put in the position of spending the better part of their consumer interviews explaining the function of Noti. Conversely, with Pearl's Toothpaste Tablet, there was no doubt as to the product and they were able to dive right into the interview process.

The brand can also give a negative connotation despite the best of intention. Our initial name, for example, was ZebraTix. Zebra because our first iteration was printed black and white bar codes, thus "Zebra,"and "Tix" was merely short for tickets. After speaking to many consumers, they conveyed that they thought of "ticks" or lyme disease. Clearly not the best association for our brand! In addition, as we migrated to the wireless device and key fobs, "pass" seemed like a better fit, so we changed the name of the company. Listen to your customers, they will always steer you in the right direction.

Are you going to have a generic or specific name?	
How will you compliment your positioning method with your branding method?	
What feedback have consumers given you about your name?	

Chapter 9

Distribution Channels

Goal:

> To learn the different methods of getting your value proposition to the customer segment.

Resources:

> Blank, S., & Dorf, B. (2012). The Startup Owner's Manual: The Step-By-Step Guide for Building a Great Company. K & S Ranch.
>
> Maurya, A. (2012). Running Lean: Iterate from Plan A to a Plan That Works (Lean Series). Sebastopol: O'Reily Media.
>
> Osterwalder, A., & Pigneur, Y. (2010). Business Model Generation. John Wiley & Sons.

The evolution of the **distribution channel** has been transformative. It used to be that you would have to go down to the general store to receive your goods. Today, the distribution channel takes many different forms and multiple functions. Lets go through the functions first that Steve Blank outlines.

5 functions of the channels of distribution

1. Awareness: The channel can make the consumer aware of the offering. The most frequent channel is via email but there are numerous examples of making you "aware" of a deal through twitter, facebook, or other social medias.

2. Evaluation: Evaluation is a brief amount of time when you can essentially play with the product prior to the actual purchase. The best example is a 30 day trial period for a product where the consumer puts in credit card information but will only be charged after this evaluation period.

3. Purchase: An offer via the internet can also be made by putting in your payment information, for example on Amazon or Apple Pay.

4. Delivery: After the purchase has been made, what once was an overnight delivery to your home or office can now be virtually downloaded to your computer or wireless device. Physical products are experiencing "instant" delivery as well through biker messaging, 3D printing, and even drone delivery.

5. After sales/customer support: Ever have a problem with your product or service? After sales can be as important as the sale itself. The consumer is most likely interacting with support because there is a problem. This interaction can either resolve that problem or can make a bad situation worse. Chat, phone support, email, and possible repairs or replacement can be determinative if the customer becomes a loyal one.

Steps for channel distribution

In identifying which is the best distribution channel to use, I have outlined 3 steps to follow.

1. Identify the product as virtual or physical. In determining the distribution of the product, first identify what type of product it is. Virtual products can be downloaded directly onto your device while a physical product must be physically delivered.

2. Understand the channel economics. Knowing the channel economics will help determine which channel to use. In other words, what is the cost of using this particular channel?

3. Understand how your competitors are delivering their product to the consumers. A new distribution channel can be transformative. Amazon began as an ecommerce site that sold books. You could always get a book at the local bookstore, but by using a new distribution channel, the internet, Amazon transformed the book selling market.

In addition, look for new disruptive distribution channels to change existing markets. How will 3D printers change the restaurant industry? How about drones? One of my students had an idea of drone delivery for any item. In his company, you could be on the soccer field, become thirsty and place an order from your local 7-Eleven for a Gatorade. You would place your order on your phone and since your phone is GPS enabled, the drink would be delivered directly to you on the soccer field, on a street corner, or anywhere else. This new, disruptive channel takes the same product, but by getting it to the consumer in a new manner, it can revolutionize the market.

Will you use a virtual or physical channel?	
How much will it this channel cost you?	
What functions will this channel serve?	
What channel does your competitor use?	
Can you improve the use of this channel? How?	

Chapter 10

Customer Relationship

Goals:

Learn how to get, keep, and grow customers.

Resources:

Blank, S., & Dorf, B. (2012). The Startup Owner's Manual: The Step-By-Step Guide for Building a Great Company. K & S Ranch.

Osterwalder, A., & Pigneur, Y. (2010). Business Model Generation. John Wiley & Sons.

Maurya, A. (2012). Running Lean: Iterate from Plan A to a Plan That Works (Lean Series). Sebastopol: O'Reily Media.

Ries, E. (2011). The Lean Startup. New York, USA: Crown Business.

The **customer relationship** is the relationship that you have with your customers. Steve Blank sums up the essentials of this relationship with three questions: how are you going to get, keep, and grow your customer base? In developing your customer base, you will lay out different hypotheses as to which are the best get, keep, and grow strategies. The most effective way to determine the efficacies of your get, keep, or grow strategies is to design experiments to be either true or false. Ash Maurya in Running Lean describes these as "falsifiable experiments." For example, if the student entrepreneur tries the "get strategy" of speaking at an event, he should have a hypothesis that reads something like this: "If I speak at this event tomorrow, by the end of the week, I will have 100 extra people that signed up for my newsletter." This will certainly be either true or false at the end of the week and will help you gauge the effectiveness of this particular get strategy.

Let's dive in a little deeper in the get, keep, and grow.

In the get category, it is important to realize that it is easier to keep and upsell existing customers than it is to get new customers. But student startups usually don't have many, if any, customers. With the advance of social media, obtaining new customers is less expensive and the reach of potential new customers has expanded due to the forces of social media as well.

SEO optimization, google ads, and facebook ads are all wonderful get strategies, as are the traditional media buys, but one of the most powerful get strategies is to establish the viral loop. There are two basic components of the viral loop.

1. Make an offer- Make an offer that is compelling enough to make the user sign up. The offer can be in a video, videoscribe, or any other means to get the user to sign up. Perhaps a 30 day free trial, or if they sign up now they get 50% off their first purchase.

2. Viral- this is the key- is your offer so compelling that users will send the offer to others and they, in turn, end up signing up, thus creating the viral loop?

As with all **viral loop** strategies, make sure to track your **customer acquisition cost** (which is simply how much it will cost you to employ these strategies in order to make the consumer buy your product). In addition, make sure to conduct only one "get" strategy at a time to gauge the effectiveness of that particular experiment and as not to skew the data. Furthermore, it is important to understand that having the individual come to your website is not enough. They must either sign in or make a purchase. Eric Reiss notes that "hits" to a site is merely a vanity metric- it feels good but the consumer failed to act. Instead, track the useful metrics like how many individuals actually spent time on the site and actually became a customer.

Once you get the consumer, look for tactics to convert that customer to other products and to make them a loyal customer; i.e., "keep" that customer. Loyalty cards, points, discounts at other retailers, and great customer service are all part of successful keep strategies. Whatever your keep strategy is, make sure that it will transform those initial consumers into raving, loyal customers. That was our loyalty component of ZebraPass. The ticket holder would go to the game using his ZebraPass. After the game, the ticket holders could go to one of the team's sponsors and flash their ZebraPass at one of our Zpads located at the sponsor's retail location. The hypothesis was that the good association of the team would transfer to the sponsor, thereby making loyal fans of the sports team loyal fans of the sponsor's product as well.

Finally, growing your customer base. For startups, the process begins by going after a select group of **early adopters** who are desperate for this solution. We then proceeded to "keep" these customers through loyalty and reward programs. There comes a point where you want to scale beyond your early adopters and implement an effective growth strategy.

You can grow your company by extending your social media campaign, entering a new market, attempting more traditional media buys, or adding an additional distribution channel to reach your consumers.

By evaluating your social media campaign, you will be able to gauge what was effective during the campaign. This is the opportunity to understand the results, fine tune them, and then make an even bigger splash in extending the campaign. In addition, you might want to try more traditional campaigns such as TV, radio, and print.

Your early adopters were a defined set of early users who shared similar characteristics and behaviors. By entering a new customer market you are going to be appealing to a larger market of potential consumers.

If your first distribution channel was, for example, the internet, it might be time to try a mobile application or enter a retail storefront or chain of stores. This will give you more visibility and extend your potential customer base.

The growth strategy entails exciting the base to expand your reach. Giveaways are nice generators of excitement, as are contests. Well designed contests are wonderful invitations to potentially new customers. Some contests are used as idea generators- such as suggest a new flavor and win X. Other contests, such as the McDonalds Monopoly giveaway, merely rewards individuals who frequent the business more by offering more chances to win, while inciting potentially new customers with a chance to win a prize. Either way, they are both excitement generators.

	Get	Keep	Grow
Strategy 1: **Acquisition Cost:** **Lifetime Value:**			
Strategy 2: **Acquisition Cost:** **Lifetime Value:**			
Strategy 3: **Acquisition Cost:** **Lifetime Value:**			

Chapter 11

Key Resources

Goals:
>   Understanding the **5 key resources**: human, financial, intellectual property, physical, and unique advantage.

Resources:
>   Blank, S., & Dorf, B. (2012). The Startup Owner's Manual: The Step-By-Step Guide for Building a Great Company. K & S Ranch.
>
>   Osterwalder, A., & Pigneur, Y. (2010). Business Model Generation. John Wiley & Sons.
>
>   Maurya, A. (2012). Running Lean: Iterate from Plan A to a Plan That Works (Lean Series). Sebastopol: O'Reily Media., United States Patent and Trademark Office. (n.d.). Retrieved July 17, 2015, from USPTO website: http://www.uspto.gov
>
>   Google Patents. (n.d.). Retrieved July 17, 2015, from Google website:
>   https://www.google.com/?tbm=pts&gws_rd=ssl
>
>   Sherman, A. J. (2011). Harvesting Intangible Assets: Uncover Hidden Revenue in Your Company's Intellectual Property. New York: AMACOM.

There are four important key resources that Blank outlines during his course, they are:
physical, financial, human, and intellectual property. Ash Maurya, in his book, *Running Lean*, discusses another key resource that he dubs "your unique advantage."

Lets discuss each of the key resources in detail.

1. *Physical Resource*

The physical resource can be your office, your manufacturing plant, or any other physical, tangible asset you may have. Quite possibly it is the manufacturing assets you have inside the plant, such as 3D printers. Your physical assets are part of your strategy. There are many decisions to be made when you set up your first office. For example, if you plan to interact with the federal government, you would place an office in the Washington, DC area. State income tax, proximity to investors, or the location of clients are all considerations one must make when setting up shop.

In addition, the cost of labor and the availability of potential hires should also be a factor when picking a location for your office.

2. *Financial Resource*

The phrase "cash is king" is very appropriate for startups. Much of what we discuss in this book is strategies to manage these costs. Even so, expenditures will occur. But not all monies received will have equal value. The investment in your company has to be evaluated based on who is making that investment. Let's take a look at the different financing options.

Many startups get their initial influx from the entrepreneur's own dollars. The entrepreneur will "boot strap" this phase through savings, credit cards, and maybe, from a prior sale. Many investors will want to see the entrepreneur dedicate not only his time toward his business, but also some of his own money.

The first level of outside investments is generally referred to as the family and friends round. Institutional investors, such as venture capitalists, will normally want to see a family and friends round before they put in their own money. After all, if your family and friends don't believe in you, why should they? Even during this preliminary round, an attorney should be consulted. There are specific SEC regulations about what net worth these investors must have, the exceptions to that rule, and the type of information that each investor must receive prior to making the investment. State regulations are likely to apply as well.

The first round of institutional investors is referred to as the series A round. Almost always, a venture capitalist will take a board position and demand that they receive preferred shares. Preferred shares means that during a liquidation event, the preferred shareholders will receive their money first, despite their equity share, then it will be shared pro rata based on equity ownership.

In order to receive venture capital money, the entrepreneur may have to change his corporate structure to permit both preferred and common shareholders. We will discuss corporate structures in another chapter.

At ZebraPass, we raised a "family and friends" round of $1 million. Though this was a family and friends round, we tried to get as many "strategic" investors as possible. This included individuals who were in the movie and sports industry. For our first round of institutional investors, the series A round, again, we looked for a strategic partner. Since we were a mobile ticketing and loyalty system company, we were looking for an investor that could help us navigate through the mobile space. Nokia Ventures seemed like the perfect investor.

As an entrepreneur, you should always remember that investors are not your friend. They have a fiduciary duty to their investors as well. This was a lesson that Jordan and I learned one night in Sonoma, California as we attended Nokia's portfolio getaway. I gave a presentation to the entire Nokia investment team. Before my presentation, the head partner reminded me a few times that we were scheduled for dinner with him and our local rep. At the time, the board consisted of two Nokia Venture members, Steven Spielberg's agent, Jordan, and myself. Our documents indicated that since Jordan and I were majority shareholders, we could appoint the next member.

During dinner and just before my big, mouthwatering filet came out, Nokia Venture's head rep came to dinner. He told us that he wanted us to appoint our current CEO to the board. He stated that since he had the most experience he would add value to the board. The reality was it was a power play. Nokia didn't want me and Jordan to have too much control of the company. We ended up relenting and we added the CEO to the board. In retrospect, we should have held our ground as he added very little to the board and I would have preferred to put a better qualified and better positioned person as board member. Student entrepreneurs- remember to always follow the documents. If you are entitled to something, don't back away from it. As the company started to wind down, it would have been great to have another business person on the board who was on our side.

I never did eat that filet.

Many companies use popular crowdfunding sites such as kickstarter and indiegogo to raise funds. At these sites, you promise to give something away, such as early access to the product, in exchange for small investments. This can be appealing because there is no exchange of equity and they can simultaneously act as an MVP because consumers can give you feedback on your product as you start to build. Unlike equity investments, these type of investments are most likely considered income, so plan accordingly.

Some companies are eligible for government and other institutional grants. As with crowdfunding, there is no equity investment so unless it fits into a very specific carved out exception, these investments are considered income as well.

In addition, there is always the traditional bank loan. Though banks are less likely to invest in a start up with no **revenue**, there are small business loans where the government will guarantee a large portion of the loan so the banks will be more inclined to make the loan. These may be appropriate once you have gained some traction and sales. Be prepared to give the bank your business plan and, since bank loans are paid back with interest, they are not considered income.

For companies that are looking for vendor financing, there are many companies that will provide vendor leases. You may find, however, that the interest rate for these leases may be 5-7% higher than you will find from the banks.

Entrepreneurs are always looking for strategic partners. Sometimes these corporate partners are not only good business fits, but they also may take an equity position in your company. This can lead to a strategic acquisition down the road as well.

Human Resources

Human resources usually fall into two categories. The first is the advisory capacity that your advisors and mentors can provide for you. Generally, a board of advisors will look out for the best interest of the entrepreneur. I counsel all of my students to make sure that they surround themselves with a strong board of advisors who can provide sound advice and be candid with the entrepreneur. The board of advisors should not be confused with the board of directors. While the board of advisors generally have the best interests of the entrepreneur at heart, the board of directors have a fiduciary duty to act in the best interests of the company. If that includes terminating the founders, then so be it.

The second human resources are your employees. Do you have that stud CTO that everyone would love to have? A big role of a young entrepreneur is attracting the very best people you can. Companies will implement strong 401k plans and other benefits to attract good people. Unfortunately, many startups simply don't have those in place yet. Therefore, great entrepreneurs are able to get good employees through sharing equity and in selling the dream. This will be a nice indicator of your concept and you, the entrepreneur. Are people jumping at the chance to join your company, or is it still just you in your mom's basement?

Co-founders are an important human resource for the business. In choosing your co-founder, it is important that you are both passionate and that you have a different skill set from one another. At ZebraPass, Jordan and I had very similar skill sets. We were both creative and good sales people. Before ZebraPass' acquisition, it turned out that Nokia Ventures had been conspiring to only bring Jordan to the new company. It was explained to me later that the acquiring company didn't need two of the same person.

In the United States Constitution; Article 1, Section 8, Clause 8, it grants Congress the power "To promote the progress of science and useful arts, by securing for limited times to authors and inventors the exclusive right to their respective writings and discoveries." The founders of our country understood the need to incentivize inventors with exclusivity, but to limit that exclusivity for a restricted time period to ensure that the society could benefit from the invention as well. There are many forms of intellectual property; patents, trademarks, copyrights, trade secrets.

Lets take a better look at each of these protections and their corresponding time grants.

Patents

A **patent** grants an inventor exclusive rights to make, use, or sell an invention for a limited period of time, generally 20 years, though different types of patents have different terms. There are three types of patents; utility, design, and business method patents. All three patents have to be filed with the United States Patent and Trademark Office.

The utility patent protects new functions of an invention or an improvement to an existing patent. A design patent protects its external appearance. Recently, Apple was awarded a large award against Samsung when the court deemed that Samsung had infringed on Apple's design patent for its iPhone. Finally, there is the business method patent, which protects the method of the business or its process. Many software companies file a business method patent. Typically, it takes 18 months for the **USPTO** to respond to your patent application.

The filing for patents can be quite expensive. A cheaper, temporary alternative is to file a provisional patent. While a full patent can cost in the many thousands of dollars, a provisional patent for micro entities is merely $65. After a provisional patent is filed, you have 1 year from that filing date to file the full patent. The benefit of a provisional patent is that the full patent application date will revert back the filing of the provisional patent date, affording the entrepreneur an earlier date of patent protection. Keep in mind, however, if you fail to file the full patent application within that one year grace period, you will lose the benefits of the provisional patent. I like provisional patents because it gives the student entrepreneur time to vet his ideas cheaply and then determine whether it makes sense to file the full application.

Copyrights

Copyrights are for creators' original work. A painting, sculpture, or novel, for example, all fall under the protection of copyright. What's interesting about copyright law, is that you are afforded the protection of the 50 year term (copyrights are good for 50 years) without registering with the USPTO. I could write a great novel and place it in my drawer and that original work is now copyrighted. Even with this allowance, most people file their copyright because it would give you de facto proof that it is your original work.

Trademark

Trademarks are used to protect the brand, marks, logos, and slogans. The term for trademark is ten years. It must be filed with the USPTO and unlike patents and copyrights, the terms can be renewed. In order for renewal to occur, you must show that the trademark has been in use.

Trademarks can be tricky - does McDonald's own that trademark for all retail? The answer is "no." If you were to copy the big mac and open a hamburger store and call it Mcdonalds (without the capital D), you would still be violating the trademark. I like to use the simple test of whether the consumer would be confused. In the scenario above, it is clear the consumer entering the new Mcdonald's would think that he was in the original retail giant. But how about if you were to open a Mcdonald's clothing store? In this case, I think you would be in a stronger position because the consumer would not be confused as to which Mcdonald's he was in.

Trade Secret

Trade secrets are the protection of methods, formulas or company's secrets. Though trade secrets are not filed with the USPTO, they can have the same value. For a trade secret to exist, the entrepreneur must attempt to keep the trade secret a secret. If the entrepreneur were to post his famous recipe online for everyone to see, then it is no longer a trade secret. There are times, however, when you want to share your trade secret to possibly a potential acquirer or partner. In those instances, an non-disclosure agreement should be used.

A non-disclosure agreement should not be confused with a non compete agreement. An NDA is generally used with people outside of the company, though not always. A non compete means than an employee cannot join another company in a similar space as the current employer. Courts generally frown upon non competes and will limit them in time and distance if they are too arduous.

In summary:

Copyright -- 50 years

Trademark -- every 10 years need to register v. common law

Patent -- 17 years after use, or years after filing- which is later

trade secret -- forever

Key Resources

Who are your human resources? How can they help you?	
What are your physical resources? How will you use them to your advantage?	
What are your financial resources?	
What intellectual property do you own?	
What is your unique advantage?	

Chapter 12

Revenue Streams

Goals:

To understand the different revenue streams and how the student entrepreneur is going to earn revenues from each customer segment.

Resources:

Blank, S., & Dorf, B. (2012). The Startup Owner's Manual: The Step-By-Step Guide for Building a Great Company. K & S Ranch.

Osterwalder, A., & Pigneur, Y. (2010). Business Model Generation. John Wiley & Sons.

Your **revenue model** is the strategy used to generate cash for the company from each specific customer segment, while pricing is the tactic used to support the specific revenue model. For example, Mercedes has traditionally targeted the more affluent customer segment with luxurious cars, thus their revenue model, or how they are going to generate cash, is high priced sales.

Recently, Mercedes has had a shift in their strategy. Though they continue to target many in their established base, they now reach out to those who traditionally have not been able to afford Mercedes. Mercedes supports this new revenue model through a pricing tactic that enables these new purchases. Thus, with the introduction of the C class series of lower priced cars, it matches Mercedes' new tactic of generating more sales from those that can now afford the cars. This has become an "entry class" of new buyers made up of young professionals who one day may opt for the more expensive, traditional Mercedes.

Determining your revenue model strategy is not an easy chore. To be discussed in more detail in future chapters, they are mere guesses until there have been opportunities to validate or invalidate the guesses through consumer interviews. In the interim, how best to make these guesses? Two good indicators are to look at current competitors. How are they pricing their products now? Which customer segment have they targeted? The second is to see how customers are currently buying the products. Are they leasing the products, or retaining it on credit? These indicators will help you shape your revenue model and ask yourself, "how can we shake up the current market?" You may have a great opportunity, even if you have a similar product as your competitor, if you have a unique revenue model that makes it easier for your targeted consumer to make the purchase.

Revenue Stream Chart

What is your competitor's revenue strategy?	
What is your revenue strategy?	
Who are you targeting with this strategy?	
How will your pricing tactic support this strategy?	
Is your strategy working? How can you make it more successful?	

Chapter 13

Cost Structures

Goals:
>   Begin to focus on profit and loss, cash burn, and customer acquisition costs.

Resources:
>   Blank, S., & Dorf, B. (2012). The Startup Owner's Manual: The Step-By-Step Guide for Building a Great Company. K & S Ranch.
>   Osterwalder, A., & Pigneur, Y. (2010). Business Model Generation. John Wiley & Sons.

Student entrepreneurs should be concerned with three cost structure statements; the profit and loss statement, cash burn, and customer acquisition cost. Many student entrepreneurs are afraid to look at their profit and loss, and with little and sometimes no revenue, I can hardly blame them. Even so, they still need to analyze their profit and loss to get a full understanding of their costs and to see what path to profitability they must take.

Every profit and loss statement is divided into revenues and **expenses**. You merely subtract gross revenues from your expenses and you will get your **net revenues**.

$$\text{Net Revenue} = \text{Gross Revenue} - \text{Expenses}$$

Expenses are further subdivided into specific categories.

The cost of goods sold are any expense that is directly related in the production of a good that is later sold. So, a factory worker at the plant to make the widget is part of the costs of goods sold because he helped produce that widget. The salesperson, however, would not be, since he did not directly make that widget. The salesperson is part of a different category called selling, general, and administrative expenses, all of which would also include management, the office, etc.

For cash burn, this needs to be monitored closely because the lack of cash is the enemy of all startups. Cash burn indicates how much the company is spending per month before it starts generating a positive cash flow. If a company has $500,000 in the bank and has a **cash burn rate** of $100,000, that means it only has 5 months before it runs out of money. Student entrepreneurs need to be cognizant of this burn rate so they can either make adjustments in their cost structures or seek further investment into the company.

The customer acquisition cost is important to gauge because you want to assess how effective your get strategy campaigns have been. With customer acquisition costs, you must also determine how long that customer stays with your company after you have spent the money to acquire him. This is generally referred to as the **lifetime value** of the consumer. For example, DirecTV ran a promotion where they would give you $100 for every customer that you referred to the company. So, the $100 was the customer acquisition for that consumer. Was this an effective campaign for DirecTV? We can only determine that once we see how long that customer stays at DirecTV. If he were to only stay with the company for $70 worth of revenue for DirecTV, then no, the lifetime value is less than the customer acquisition costs and it would not be worth it. But if the customer were to stay with DirecTV to the point that it earned over $1,000 in revenue, then yes, the campaign was worth it. DirecTV could then look back at this get strategy and see that it was indeed an effective campaign.

At ZebraPass, we had raised over $5 million in angel and venture capital money. One of the most exciting days in my life was the day that Nokia Ventures wired in over $4 million into our account.

How did we spend the money? We hired like crazy, had fancy new digs, and threw everything at the wall to see what would stick. Instead of every month trying to determine our cash burn to control costs, Nokia made sure we ramped up and got as many clients as possible. There was no real strategic usage of our cash. It was, so clearly, a poor business model.

Things we should have done:
1. determine our remaining cash burn rate at the end of every month.
2. focus on one trial- set up metrics and determine what was working and what was not working
3. stay lean- keep the software we had already created from digital focus
4. not hire so many people

In short, we should have sparingly used our cash and learned first before we spent.

Profit and Loss Template

Total Income	
Income from Sales	
Income from Services	
Other income	
Total Expenses	
Get, Keep, Grow Strategies	
Price of production	
Other Expenses	
Net Income (Total Income - Total Expenses)	

Chapter 14

Key Partnerships

Goal:
> Understanding the benefits of a successful partnership.

Resources:
> Blank, S., & Dorf, B. (2012). The Startup Owner's Manual: The Step-By-Step Guide for Building a Great Company. K & S Ranch.
>
> Osterwalder, A., & Pigneur, Y. (2010). Business Model Generation. John Wiley & Sons.

Every student entrepreneur has to determine who to partner with to help them succeed. Student entrepreneurs should focus on partnerships that can either help with speed to market, or a strategic relationship that can lead to a future acquisition.

Speed to market

There are many variations of **speed to market** partnerships. At the Georgetown University Summer launch program, for example, there is one team, Sunniva LLC, that is going to launch its healthy, cold coffee product in one Whole Foods store. If this pilot is successful, Whole Foods might potentially put them in hundreds of stores, thus increasing their speed to market through a larger distribution partnership.

Partnerships also allow you to focus on your core offering while outsourcing smaller tasks to other companies that may already have that expertise. For example, Intel partners with many computer companies to provide the necessary computer chips. It's entirely possible that the computer companies, if they spent enough money on research and development, could develop their own chip. But why go through the expense when Intel already does it well?

Allowing Intel to provide the chips saves these companies money and it allows them to focus on their core offering.

Moreover, as you begin to scale, you may look to partner with your vendor to help lower costs. This will help you enter the market more quickly as well.

Potential Acquirer

These strategic partners are generally the big players in the same space. Your core offering is something that complements theirs. This partner may want to acquire you to absorb your customers or to ensure that your offering becomes theirs, exclusively.

There are of course risks inherent with some partnerships. Let's assume you outsource part of your offering and the partner does a poor job on their end. It's your brand still on the product so that could hurt the brand and your company's reputation.

Exclusive partnerships seem good on their face, but they may hurt your potential growth. These are important considerations when entering a partnership. It is important to weigh the costs and benefits of every partnership carefully before entering into that particular partnership.

Partnership Chart

Is this partner a potential acquirer or will they help with speed to market?	
How specifically will they help?	
What smaller tasks can they perform for you?	
What are the strengths and weaknesses of your partner? How do they complement your team's strengths and weaknesses?	

Chapter 15

Customer Development

Goal:

> Understanding that all learning comes from outside of the building.

Resources:

> Blank, S., & Dorf, B. (2012). <u>The Startup Owner's Manual: The Step-By-Step Guide for Building a Great Company</u>. K & S Ranch.
>
> Maurya, A. (2012). <u>Running Lean: Iterate from Plan A to a Plan That Works (Lean Series)</u>. Sebastopol: O'Reily Media.
>
> Ries, E. (2011). <u>The Lean Startup</u>. New York, USA: Crown Business.

Customer development is essential to developing a product that you know your consumer will desire. Steve Blank indicates that customer development has 4 phases: identifying the problem, testing the problem, testing the solution, and then pivoting or iterating. Eric Reiss sets up a "Build-Test-Measure-Pivot or Persevere" loop. They both indicate that there are no facts in the building and that customer development occurs outside of the classroom. In fact, they say to spend 15 to 20 minutes setting up your business model canvas and to spend the rest of the time on customer discovery. Though I agree that most of the work is done outside of the building by carefully crafted interviews and through true learning from consumers to find a solution, I think the student entrepreneur should spend a significant amount of time at the onset thinking through the business model canvas and placing their hypotheses down on the canvas. Through brainstorming and other design thinking techniques discussed earlier, student entrepreneurs will have a stronger foundation to begin the process. But it is only the beginning. Your hypotheses are now on the business model canvas and it is time to validate or invalidate these hypotheses by performing customer interviews.

During customer discovery, we suggest a series of targeted, focused interviews to test the hypotheses on your business model canvas. After each set of interviews, you should be able to answer these simple questions:

1. What was my hypothesis?
2. What questions did I ask?
3. What did I learn?
4. What is my hypothesis now?
5. What I am going to do next?

In addition, you should be focusing in on one hypothesis for the week. That should be the one component that you are measuring for the week, so test it and validate or invalidate it. In addition, each week's group of customers should be labeled in their own cohort. A **cohort** is a group treated the same. It's important to put them in such cohorts because as your product changes, you may want to go back to the consumers with additional questions on your pivots. What the product looked like in week 1 will be vastly different in week 6. In addition, even though we are focusing in on one hypothesis, Diana Kander, a NY Times bestseller author and successful entrepreneur, suggests to have open ended questions. This gives the customer the opportunity to expand on the topic and to give you insightful feedback on what they would like to see in your product.

Problem Interviews

The first interviews to be conducted are the problem interviews. The consumer is only concerned about his problem, not your solution. This is your opportunity to really discover their problems. In addition, we are trying to determine if there is even a problem that exists and if it is a problem that the interviewee wants solved. There are varying degrees of consumer's problems. In other words, does the consumer scream "I have this problem," or is it a quiet whisper, "yea, that happens sometimes." The problem that screams out is the one that needs to be solved.

On a side note, I am not a strong supporter of surveys and much prefer face to face interviews. You can look into their eyes to determine veracity, ask follow up questions, and develop a rapport with a potential customer, things you can never do with a survey. In addition, you can measure behavior a lot more effectively through observation then through a survey.

When conducting these interviews, you want to have a basic script whereby you can collect demographics on the interviewee and have a set list of questions. This way you can compare apples to apples over a series of interviews. When identifying the problem, try to determine how the customer is solving the problem now. Is it an ad hoc solution he has developed on their own, or is it an off the shelf solution? How can we start to differentiate your solution from the existing ones already out there? Finally, always ask for 2-3 people the interviewees might refer your way, that is a great resource for additional interviews.

Solution Interviews

The second set of interviews are the solution interviews, or essentially, the value proposition interviews. During this time, you should be able to show your interviewees a low fidelity prototype. The prototype can be in programs such as balsamiq or justinmind or they can use a simple slide deck from a powerpoint presentation. The potential consumer should be able to sample the consumer experience, or at least see what it might be, and provide comments from there. In essence, this is customer collaboration. Previously we worked hard to discover the problem, now we are working with the customer to iterate and find a solution that works for them.

Customization Interviews

During these rounds of interviews, you are looking to customize your low fidelity prototype to the customer. For example, if the presentation is to your high school, include the school colors on it. Try to discover how this product can be unique to them and if there are other customization features they would like to see in your product.

Expert Interviews

Student entrepreneurs must identify and interview 3-5 experts within the product's industry. There is real value in determining who the thought leaders are within the targeted industry, and to get their insight. These experts might also later serve on your board of advisors or become investors in your company.

I can remember my first expert interview. It was with the head of Paramount Studios and we were trying to learn about movie studios to see if they would potentially become a customer of ZebraPass. Sue Spielberg and I walked into Paramount Studios to meet with the President of Paramount. We were shown to his office and sat down. I looked on the wall and there was a picture of the president of the studio with his arm around Sue's brother, Steven Spielberg. I bumped my elbow into Sue's arm, pointed to the picture and whispered into her ear, "this is going to be easy."

I looked over at the president. His feet were up on the desk and he was reading the newspaper. he continued to read his paper and didn't acknowledge us for what seemed like an eternity, though it was probably more like 5 minutes or so. Sue and I both became antsy in our seats. Finally, someone else came in to break the silence. This person worked for the president of Paramount and was not thrilled to see us.

"Ah man! Is this the theater ticketing thing spearheaded by that jerk? I need this like I need a hole in my head."

"No, we are not from the theaters," I clarified. I was confused by his comment; I was always under the assumption that the theaters and the studios worked together, so why would he have been so bothered? I learned quickly that assumptions about business relationships should be investigated, and that listening was potentially more important than talking. I initially thought I was there to discuss our ticketing solution but quickly discovered that these types of conversations were so much more productive when I actually listened and really got a better understanding of*their* problems. And here was their problem; apparently, the theaters had banded together to set up a ticketing company. At the time, moviefone was making all the money in the ticket service business. Here was another interesting tidbit. Studios made 90% of revenues the first week that a movie was released to the theaters, and then it was a sliding scale from there.

The longer that the movie was in the theater, the percentage share for the theater increased. Now you know why popcorn costs so much. Here was another opportunity for the theaters to make money.

There was another interesting thing we learned, theaters were not united in their fight for controlling the ticketing dollars. There was one group, led by the founder of Hollywood.com and National Amusements, calling their company movietickets.com and the the second group, which was and of the majority of theaters, calling their new ticketing group fandango.

From this interview, we were able to understand the the studio's perspective and the animosity that existed between theater and studios. We also learned about potential ticketing competitors in Fandango and movietickets.com and we could adjust our strategy to become their potential partner as opposed to their foe. After this meeting we changed ZebraPass from being the front end,where our brand was selling tickets, to being the back end technology, to potentially support and partner with Fandango and Movietickets. This was a monumental pivot that only transpired after learning the *problem*. Now, we just had to convince one of them to take a chance on us.

Pricing Interviews

Student entrepreneurs in this week's set of interviews will validate different types of pricing. Each Student entrepreneur should test a minimum of 3 different pricing hypothesis with 10-15 interviews. It is also important to support every revenue model with a supporting pricing tactic. If you are selling Rolls Royces and the strategy is to sell to the affluent, the price should be reflective of that (and not sell the car for $5,000 but $100,000 to hit the right customer segment).

Distribution interviews

By this point, you have guessed what the most efficient distribution channel is. Now it is time to see if the customers agree with you. In this week's set of interviews, test at least 2 different types of distribution channels and see if you are really reaching the customer that wants to be reached.

Competitor Interviews

In this week's set of interviews, the focus should be on the competitors' solutions. Try to ascertain what features consumers like about these products and go back and try to improve upon them.

High Fidelity Interviews

By now, you should have received a lot of feedback on your product. It is time to refine your demo and turn it into a functional prototype that gives the consumer as close to the real experience as possible.

Cohorts and Pivots interviews

Bring your high fidelity prototype to 2 of the existing cohorts you had previously interviewed. The high fidelity prototype should be very different from the original offering. Are they still interested? Are they more interested than they were originally, or did you lose them with the changes?

Viral loop Test

Though not an interview, the students will spend significant time on improving their facebook pages and twitter accounts in an effort to get as many potential consumers as possible through the viral loop.

Interview Chart

Demographics of Interviewee	Age: Gender: Interests: Email/Phone number: Other information:
Hypothesis you are testing	
Questions you asked	
What you learned	

Chapter 16

Competitive Analysis

Goals:
>To learn how to set up a competitive analysis and to have a tool kit of analysis to use to evaluate the competition.

Resources:
>Maurya, A. (2012). Running Lean: Iterate from Plan A to a Plan That Works (Lean Series). Sebastopol: O'Reily Media.
>Porter, M. "The Five Competitive Forces that Shape Strategy", Harvard Business Review, January 2008, p.86-104.

A good friend of mine, Jon, was a graduate of the Stanford business school and therefore received the Stanford newsletter. He came across a new company started by Stanford students called Just Arrive, that used RFID technology in their turnstiles in order to print out tickets. Their turnstile solution was a lot more elegant than ours and one of their main investors was Ronnie Lott, a well recognized sports figure in the Bay area turned investor. His affiliation to Just Arrive was a potential stumbling block; it could diffuse some of our "unique advantage" of having sport figures as investors attached to ZebraPass. What was a little strange was that Ronnie Lott's business partner, Harris Barton, also a former football player, had already invested in our company!

What did we do with this information? We did nothing. I mean nothing. Didn't reach out to them, and didn't interview any customers that potentially could use their product. We simply ignored it. A cardinal sin that students should not repeat.

There are two steps to take when analysing a competitor. The first step is to set up an analysis using basic competitive analysis tools; competitive analysis, environmental analysis, and five force analysis. At the high school level, we combine this into one simple report so it is one piece of paper that allows you to easily discern where your competitor stands.

The second step is to interview the competitor's customers to discover what is working and what is not working. Also, this helps you differentiate your offering from the competitors. You will find what Ash Maurya calls your "unique advantage."

A simple competitive analysis will help you identify your competitors and at the very least learn about their revenues, their market share, and their partners. An effective comparative analysis will then tie in the environment that exists for your product and the five forces that dictate the market.

An environmental analysis will include any demographic shifts, socio economic changes, new technology trends, and political legislation that may shape the competitive landscape. For example, Uber came across many legislative obstacles and lobbying efforts from the taxi unions for nearly every market they entered. Uber was able to use this hostile environment and turn it into a marketing opportunity. It was the understanding of the environment that helped shape their business model.

In a five force analysis, you look at five different factors to help gauge the competition:

1. Number of competitors in the market
   a. The fewer the competitors, the more appealing the market. A whole host of competitors normally means that as a group, they will drive down the cost because of the competitive nature of the segment.

2. Threat of new entrants
   a. Is it easy for new entrants to enter the market? If it is difficult, that makes a market more appealing as once you have entered the market, other potential competitors will find it difficult to enter the same market. The impediments could include legislation barriers, technology lock ins, or monetary lock ins.

In addition, if there is an enormous sunk cost to enter that market, this may help deter potential competitors from entering the market, especially if that sunk cost can only be used for their current business. This acts as a barrier because should that business fail, that sunk cost cannot be used again because it only has one use, for that failed business. If, however, that sunk cost could be used for a different venture, then there would be less of a barrier because the investor is hedging his bet; even if the business fails, he can use that sunk cost for another venture.

3. Threat of substitutes or additional complements
    a. Is it easy for a product similar to yours entering the market? Although it is not identical to yours, is yours easily substituted for this new product? For example, peanut oil and sunflower oil are very similar products. The definitive question to ask is, will consumers use each of these two products interchangeably? If there is an increase in the cost of sunflower oil, will it drive the consumers to use the peanut oil instead, merely because it is cheaper? If so, then this threat of the substitute product should be treated as a competitor even though you may not have initially cited them as a competitor because their product is slightly different.

A complement to your product is an ancillary benefit to the consumer but does not replace the actual product. For example, microsoft added software to other computers that help run your company. This software never sought to replace the computer. In fact, it was dependent upon that product (the personal computer) for selling its own software product and is therefore an additional complement.

4. Power of suppliers
    a. If there are only a few suppliers, they can set the price because there are only a few alternatives. If there are a lot of suppliers, the product will compete to get your business and you will be more likely to negotiate a better price.

5. Power of Buyers
   a. As with suppliers, the more buyers the better so long as you are not included in that lot. The buyers will have the power if there are fewer of them.

It is important to gather all of this information to really understand your competitors and to start to differentiate your offering.

Competitors Chart

Number of competitors in your market	
Who are these competitors? What do they do well? What do they do poorly?	
Threat of new entrants to the market	
Can you establish any barriers to entry for your product?	
Threat of substitutes or additional complements to your product	
Power of suppliers (can you find a large amount of suppliers)	
Power of buyers (Can you find a large amount of buyers)	

Chapter 17

Corporations

Goals:

To understand the different types of corporations and which ones are best suitable for a startup.

Resources:

Sherman, A. J. (2011). Harvesting Intangible Assets: Uncover Hidden Revenue in Your Company's Intellectual Property. New York: AMACOM.

There are many types of corporations to choose from and determining which is best for your company depends on several factors including the stage of the company, fundraising needs, and tax consequences. It is also important for liability purposes to incorporate and to safeguard yourself in case of future litigation. Just be careful to fulfill all the requirements of whatever corporate structure you choose, or other entities or persons may try to pierce the corporate "veil," thereby denying you the liability protection you want.

Each of the corporate structures afford the members insulation from liability if specific steps are taken. Lets take a look at the specific types and describe their corresponding characteristics.

1. Limited Liability Company- "LLC"

For the LLC, there is a controlling document that discusses income allocation, ownership, meeting requirements, and operating procedures. This document is called the "operating agreement." What's interesting about the operating agreement is that income distribution can be different than ownership, as long as it is clearly spelled out in the operating agreement. That notion is unlike the S and C corporations where distribution must also be based on ownership. For example, Owner A owns 75% of the LLC while Owner B owns only 25%. If the operating agreement states that Owner B can receive 90% of the profits despite the fact that he only owns 25% of the LLC, that is completely permissible in an LLC.

There are other advantages to an LLC as well. There is no formal requirement to have board meetings or to record minutes as is required in S and C corporations. Moreover, the taxes flow to the individual members as opposed to the corporation which avoids the double taxation scenario.

The disadvantage of an LLC is that there is only one class of members. Venture capitalists will almost certainly require preferred shares and thus typically do not invest in an LLC.

2. S Corp

The S corporation has many similarities as an LLC, but also has some differences. It has common shareholders, officers and directors, and must meet formal requirements such as board meetings and keep records of minutes from each board meeting. Here are some of the characteristics of an S corp;

a. up to 100 common shareholders
b. taxation flows onto personal tax return (same as an LLC)
c. the operator must take a salary that meets the industry standard
d. income allocation must be distributed by shareholder percentage, unlike an LLC where the operating agreement determines income distribution.

3. C corporation

A C corp is the option insisted upon by most venture capitalists. It has very formal requirements in that there is a board of directors which meet periodically and minutes must be kept outlining what occurred in those meetings. Though the CEO may be on the board of directors, the board is required to set the vision for the company while the management team are the actual day to day operators of the company. Board members do have a fiduciary duty to act in the best interests of the company.

There are two classes of shareholders in a C corp, the common shareholder and the preferred shareholder. The preferred shareholder has liquidation preference and venture capitalists who invest in your company will almost certainly take preferred shares.

C corps are not ideal for small business due to their double taxation. For example, if company A is a C corp, it will be taxed on profits and again on distributions, a provision known as double taxation.

All corporate structures must receive a tax ID number from the state in which they incorporate,and receive a federal tax ID number known as an EIN number.

Which corporation is best suitable for your company?	
What features attract you to this specific corporation?	

Chapter 18

Ethics

Goals:
To learn how business can be both profitable and ethical.

My brother-in-law loves to tell me jokes. One in particular set off a nice ethical dilemma that many young student entrepreneurs may find themselves contemplating.

It goes something like this: there are two salesmen who head to a poor region in the Dominican Republic. When they arrive to the small town of 10,000 people, they both notice that none of the inhabitants are wearing shoes. The first salesman hops on the next plane home and says to his boss, "no opportunity, no one wears shoes."

The second salesman hops on his cell phone, very excited and calls his boss, "send 10,000 pairs of shoes, lots of opportunity." Which brings us to the ethical dilemma scenario we like to set up for the student entrepreneur.

The town becomes such a purchaser of shoes that they set up a shoe manufacturing plant that provides many jobs for the townspeople and sells shoes at a very reasonable price. The problem is that the average wage in Dominican Republic is $5 per hour, significantly less than the same wage workers would get in the United States. Now it is time to compare the Dominican Republic company (let's call it the DR) to two other companies to see which is the most ethical.

The first company we will use for comparison is Toms shoes. Their business model is to provide a free pair of shoes for every shoe purchased. The other shoe company is Gideon Shoes, where all shoes are made in Australia to ensure a fair wage. Moreover, this company donates a portion of their profits to charity. Most of their shoes sell in the range of $120 to $300 a pair.

On its face, the Dominican Republic company seems like the least ethical due to the low wages. But haven't they now provided jobs where there once were none? Unlike Toms where they merely give away one pair of shoes per pair purchased, the DR company employs individuals so that workers can buy their own shoes and earn money to provide food for their family. How about Gideon shoes, the company that gives away part of their profits and employs people at fair wages? Well, since Gideon shoe products are for the more affluent and sell at that high price range, the company has low sales, the profit share does not have a great impact, and because it is a luxury brand, there is not much of a social impact that translates to providing footwear to those in need.

I am not arguing that below average wages are ethical. I am merely suggesting that all circumstances must be looked at when judging what is "ethical and unethical." I would argue that in the end, jobs are the most ethical and beneficial contribution that an entrepreneur can provide to society.

Chapter 19

Analytics

Goals:
> Learn to track information and to stay focused on the key data for the week.

Resource:
> Croll, A., & Yoskovitz, B. (2013). Lean Analytics: Use Data to Build a Better Startup Faster (Lean Series). O'Reilly Media.
>
> Maurya, A. (2012). Running Lean: Iterate from Plan A to a Plan That Works (Lean Series). Sebastopol: O'Reily Media.

There is so much information out there, along with a ton of tracking tools, that it remains imperative for student entrepreneurs to stay focused. In collecting data, there are some wonderful tools, with the most common used being Google Analytics Official Website – Web Analytics & Reporting. It is amazing to see who comes to your website and for how long. But be careful. Don't measure the mere fact that people are coming to your site. Rather, you should track the conversion rate of those merely visiting your site, to those that become active users by either signing in or making a purchase. This will help you stay focused on who is really interested in seeing their problem solved.

As set forth in customer development, it is also important to gauge one metric per week. In other words, what learning can the entire team focus in on and gain new insights from, by the end of the week. This will help keep the team focused and on the same page and moving forward.

In collecting data, there are two types of data we will focus on, qualitative and quantitative. What's the difference? Qualitative is the feedback you will get from the customer interviews, more anecdotal than anything. There is a tremendous amount of learning that comes from qualitative feedback. I use quantitative, on the other hand, as the empirical support that there is an actual market for this idea.

In assessing an idea, many student entrepreneurs are tempted to go after the low hanging fruit and test the easiest assumption first. Maurya says it best in Running Lean: attack the riskiest assumption first. In our Georgetown University Summer launch program there was one student entrepreneur company called Anybox. Their hypothesis was that office buildings wanted to have vending machines on the first floor with healthier options. The founder wanted to test his food in a farmer's market because that was the easiest place to start the testing. But the farmer's market attendees were not his target market. Even if they loved the food, he still wouldn't have proven that office people wanted to purchase his healthy options. His first step should have been to go into as many office buildings as possible, offer them samples, and then see if one, just one, would let him set up a table on the first floor and sell his food for one lunch period. In other words, he had to test the hypothesis that office people wanted to eat his healthier options. The vending machine would come later.

Don't be afraid of failure during these times. It may seem ok to gain confidence getting that initial "confirmation," but that is not what student entrepreneurs should be looking for. It is the learning that they should be seeking, not confirmation. Analytics will help you with this learning by tracking how far you have come, as well as pointing you in the direction you need to go.

Analytics Chart

Qualitative	
Interviewees reaction to the product. Would they use it?	
Are they using any ad hoc solutions now? If so, how are they solving the problem?	
What did you learn from the qualitative analytics? Does it validate or invalidate your hypothesis?	
Quantitative	
What empirical data did you collect?	

Chapter 20

Leadership

Goal:
To adapt the qualities of a good leader.

Resource:
Hill, N. (1987). Think and Grow Rich. New York: Fawcett Books,

Maxwell, J. C. (2004). The 17 Indisputable Laws of Teamwork. Nashville: Thomas Nelson Publishers.

Student entrepreneurs are the founders of their own company and therefore must develop qualities to ensure that they will be able to recruit employees in the future. Some of these student entrepreneurs are so charismatic that they have recruited fellow students to act as interns. There are a few basic characteristics that I have noticed from coaching many student entrepreneurship teams. Below are the five characteristics that I think really stand out as leadership traits.

Leaders are Decisive

The first is to be decisive. You and your team are going to have a limited amount of resources and time. You have to make decisions and make them quickly about which direction you and your team should head. It is important to be agile and to use the advantage that since you are a small company, you have the ability to make quick decisions.

Leaders Listen and Communicate

The second trait is to listen and communicate learning. There are times that all good leaders really listen to those around them to help make their decision. Listening makes sure that everyone feels a part of the team, and that each voice is being heard. Moreover, by listening to not just your team members but to your potential customers, you are developing a product that the consumer actually wants, not what you think they want. All good listeners, in turn, communicate their thoughts and their decisions to make sure that the entire team is on the same page.

Leaders Inspire

The third ability is to inspire. No one wants to follow someone that puts them in the doldrums. In order to inspire, you must be passionate in what you are doing and have the belief that you can succeed.

"Whether you think you can, or think you can't, you're right," said Henry Ford, September, 1947 in "The Reader's Digest." It is this belief and passion that will help guide you and your team through difficult times. The student entrepreneur is meant to discover and learn from the customer. It can be discouraging to hear over and over again that they want something different than what you thought they would like. Stay positive, and make sure to keep your team in good spirits. One team in the capstone, Bonfire, came to school showing everyone an article on a company called Wigo that had a similar value proposition and had already received funding. At first they were a little disappointed by the news, but they quickly regained momentum. They realized that this showed validation for their concept and that Wigo could essentially act as an MVP for them. They could learn from the consumers that were using Wigo about what they liked, and therefore learned how they could make Bonfire even better.

Leaders Delegate

Good leaders are those that can delegate tasks and responsibilities. Many student entrepreneurs try to take on too many tasks at once. This results in the entrepreneur being inefficient and slows down company growth. They feel that if they are not doing it, then it is not being done right. I require the student teams to hold a fictional board meeting every week where one member is the chairman of the board. That chairperson then assigns tasks and focuses the team on the one metric that is going to be the focus for the week. This teaches the student entrepreneur the ability to delegate. The chairperson is also responsible for making sure that everyone did their assigned tasks properly that week.

Leaders are Fair and Resolve Conflict

Finally, student entrepreneur leaders must be fair to all other members of the team. It is important to give credit to others when merited, and to make them shine as much as possible. You want all the members of your team to feel rewarded for a job well done, and for them to feel that they are being treated well. This is great practice for when you have real employees who want to be recognized for their accomplishments. Recognizing such accomplishments will result in more motivated employees and a more charismatic company.

In addition, leaders don't let unresolved issues fester. During the capstone class this year, the eventual winning team, HotSocks, had many conflicting personalities. In one of their board meetings, two of the four students were bickering about how to position their product. A third student intervened, discussed how best to solve the issue, put it to a vote, and the issue was resolved. The team wasted no further time on this issue. They heeded her advice and their board meetings in the future were a lot more productive.

Leaders Lead by Example

All good leaders not only delegate the work, but they are actively involved in the process. It helps to keep the other students engaged when the active leader is there, side by side, participating with them in doing the work.

Board Meeting agenda

Previous week's tasks	
This week's tasks	
Delegation (Which team member will do which task)	
Checklist (Were all tasks completed)	

Chapter 21

Public Speaking

Goal:
Learn how to give effective presentations.

Resources:
Delinsky, Andrew. The Head of School, The Peck School

All student entrepreneurs at one point or another will be making presentations. Whether it is the weekly "lessons learned" presentation in front of their classmates, or making their pitches to potential investors or their next big client, it is important to be able to master the art of speaking in front of groups. Trust me, public speaking is something that will improve over time as you practice. All speakers are nervous. That's ok, it shows that you care. Here are a few guidelines when speaking that I have found to be effective in your lead up to your next big presentation.

Student Entrepreneur Speakers are Prepared

There are few feelings worse in the world than not being prepared to speak. I remember sitting in Tort's class in law school. It was parent's visiting day and the teacher was using the syncratic method and calling upon the student right next to me. I had not read the previous night's reading, and was sweating profusely hoping beyond all hope that he would not call on me. Fortunately, he never did and I was spared the embarrassment of being unprepared. I learned a valuable lesson, to always be prepared! It will spare you a lot of the anxiety and will enable you to answer the questions that are going to follow after your presentation.

Student Entrepreneurs Hook the Audience

Venture capitalists, customers, and basically all of us, have sat through numerous presentations. Break the ice a little, get the audience involved, work the crowd with a funny story or a personal little anecdote. It is always interesting to learn something new about the speaker. In short, don't be boring. You have a limited time period to engage. Do it from the start.

Student Entrepreneurs use Persuasive Language

In many cases, the student entrepreneurs are introducing a product into a new market or trying to convince the audience that their product is better than the established leader. This is the time for the active voice, to excite the audience of the possibility and to include the audience in that excitement. It is the audience that is going to benefit from this product, make them excited to be part of that process.

Student Entrepreneurs use their Body Effectively

There is nothing more drab than watching speakers that act robotic in their deliverance. Move! Use your hands, express the passion you feel for the product that you have been working on so diligently! Moreover, engage the audience. A study from the National Training Laboratories in 2000 found that people will retain 5% of the information presented if they stay seated and passively listen to a lecture, 50% will be retained if they participate in a discussion, and a whopping 70% will be retained if they engage their body and practice by doing ("Rethinking the Classroom: Spaces,") . Make your audience move, have them do workshops, brainstorm together, or merely just make them stand up. They will, in turn, absorb more of the information you are presenting.

Student Entrepreneurs Make Eye Contact

There is something to be said when you can look someone in the eye and deliver a speech. They will trust you more and they will feel more engaged. The student entrepreneur should not stay focused on just one individual, you don't want to appear "creepy," just engaged.

Student Entrepreneurs are Experts in their Subject Matter

Student entrepreneurs need to be experts in their subject matter. That means a strong understanding of their competitors, where their space is headed, and all of the nuances within their market. They must have a command as to who their customer is and the market potential for their product. They will gain expertise through the numerous interviews they will have conducted, thereby getting real feedback from their customers. They will also have empirical data to back up their assertions.

Student Entrepreneurs Give the Audience a "Take Away"

This falls in the "what can the audience do after your talk?" category. Can they sign up for your blog to learn more information? Can they actually make a purchase of your product? Perhaps there is going to be a follow up where they can volunteer to be interviewed for your concept. Something ought to be offered so that the connection you've developed from the talk does not evaporate after they walk out the doors. Remember, you are always seeking to develop that social connection with your audience, lets take advantage of it.

Public Speaking Checklist

Portion of Public Speaking	Yes/No
Do you have a hook to capture your audience? What is it?	
Do you use persuasive language? What facts and words will you use to support your points?	
Have you practiced your body movements? Are they too robotic or are they fluid?	
Do you make eye contact when you speak?	
Are you an expert in your subject? Are there areas that you need to study more?	
Are you prepared?	

Glossary of Bolded Terms

Brainwriting - an alternative to brainstorming that allows all members of the group to be involved. A group member will place an idea that solves a problem on a piece of paper and pass it to another group member. The second group member then adds onto or changes the idea and the process continues.

Business model canvas - a dynamic document from Alexander Osterwalder that helps startups map out their business model with the nine basic building blocks of businesses such as customer segment, revenue streams and value proposition.

Cash Burn Rate - how much money the company is spending per month before it starts to generate a positive cash flow.

Cohort - a certain group or segment of customers.

Copyright - for creators of an original work (i.e., a painting, novel, sculpture, etc.). Protected for 50 years even without registering it with the USPTO.

Customer Acquisition Cost - the cost associated with obtaining a new customer. For example, if Company A advertises to Jeff for $30 and he becomes a customer, the customer acquisition cost would be $30.

Customer Development - the process of validating or invalidating your company's hypoteses to further understand who your customers are and what they want. Customer Development has four phases:
a.   identifying the problem
b.   testing the problem
c.   testing the solution
d.   pivoting or iterating

Customer Relationship - the relationship you have with your customers that are based on three questions. How are you going to get customers? How are you going to keep customers? How are you going to grow your customer base?

Customer Segment - who you are going to sell your product to.

Distribution Channel - the way you get to your product to the consumer. Serves 5 main functions:
 a. Spreads awareness
 b. Evaluation - allows consumer to "trial" the product
 c. Purchase - allows consumers to pay for the product
 d. Delivery - allows for easy delivery of your product
 e. Allows for after sales contact and customer support

Early Adopters - a defined set of early users who have a passion for your product.

Expenses - the money the company spends (such as cost of goods, employee wages, etc.).

Hypothesis - an educated guess that startups will test to pinpoint characteristics of their business. For example, Company A may have a hypothesis that states that teens are their customer segment, but may disprove this hypothesis and learn that their new customer segment is actually young adults.

Ideation - a creative process for generating a large number of business ideas and then filtering them to the best ones. A good way of doing this is by filling a board with post-it notes that contain business ideas. Fill out as many post-its as possible, then remove the bad ones from the board.

Immersion - a method of brainstorming a business that involves placing yourself in your consumer's shoes and observing their behavior.

Lean Canvas - similar to the business model canvas. Used in this book to supplement the business model canvas.

Lifetime Value - the profit a customer will bring in after they are initially acquired.

Market Types - Your product will be entering one of the four following markets:

a. Clone market - Bringing an already existing product to a new place. For example, bringing KFC to China.

b. An existing market - You know the customers and the already established competitors.

c. Segmented Market - A product that is moving into an already existing market, but segments it in a certain way. For example if a new company called Apple Kids was founded and started segmenting apple products specifically for young kids.

d. New Market - You are a brand new product and are thus entering an entirely new market where the customers and competitors are unknown.

Minimum Viable Product (MVP) - the value proposition that consumers are willing to pay for on day one. The MVP allows the startup to test their product quickly while avoiding superfluous expenses on features the consumer may not want.

Net Revenue - the revenue your company makes after expenses are taken out (net revenue = gross revenue - expenses).

Patent - a patent grants an inventor exclusive rights to make, use, or sell an invention for a limited period of time, generally 20 years, though different types of patents have different terms. Patents must be filed with the USPTO.

Potential Acquirer - a type of partnership in which the person(s) or company you partner with are generally the "big players" in the same space and therefore may be able to absorb or buy you out in the future.

Product Market Fit - assuring that the value proposition fits the correct customer segment. For example, a mobile application for senior citizens would not be a good product market fit as senior citizens are generally less tech savvy.

Product Positioning - the method of portraying your product in a way that is memorable and will result in the consumer desiring your product more than your competitor's. There are basic steps to position your product:

a. Simplify your message - Simply state what your product does and why your consumer would want it.

b. Social connection - Develop a social connection with your consumers to ensure loyalty and satisfaction.

c. Position your product the way you see it - Portray your product the way you see it and the way you want others to see it as well. For example, Mercedes being a higher end vehicle than a Toyota.

d. Reposition the competitor - Point out the negative aspects of your competitor. For example, in the same scenario as above, Toyota can point out that Mercedes are too expensive and not practical.

e. Know your ranking - If you are ranked the best company in your market, do not mention the competitors.

Revenue Model - the strategy used to generate cash for the company from each specific customer segment.

Revenue Stream - how the company makes money from their customer segment.

Revenue - income of a company.

Roles of Consumers - There are 4 types of consumers in the market:

a. The user - The individual that will actually use the product.

b. The influencer - The individual that influences the user to use the product.

c. The saboteur - The individual that attempts to stop the purchase.

d. The economic buyer - The individual that will actually purchase the product (may or may not be the user).

Societal Gain - categorized as either the functional, social, or emotional gains for the user that allows them to connect with others.

Speed to Market - a type of partnership in which the person(s) or company you partner with will help bring your product to market faster than you could alone.

Trademark - used to protect brand, marks, logos, and slogans. Protection for ten years as long as it is filed with the USPTO and can be renewed as long as there is proof that the trademarked logo has been used.

Trade Secret - protection of methods, formulas, or company's secrets. These are kept forever as long as the company attempts to keep the secret.

USPTO - United States Patent and Trademark Office

Value Proposition - the value of your product. It answers one of the following three basic questions:
Does your product solve a problem?
Does it fulfill a social need?
What job does the consumer want done?

Viral Loop - important "get" strategy under customer relationship. This strategy involves using social media outlets to have others spread the word about your product.

4As of Association - the 4 laws for developing a good team and developing successful leadership. They include aspiring for something greater, acquiring great people, assessments in place, and accountability.

5 Key Resources - there are five key resources that all startups have that can give them a unique advantage:
a.   Physical - your office, manufacturing plant, store, etc.

b. Financial - the money your startup has and can use
c. Human - advisors to and employees of the company
d. Intellectual property - trademarks, trade secrets, copyrights, and patents
e. Unique advantage - not defined in the book — see chapter 10

Made in the USA
Middletown, DE
27 October 2017